The
Canberra Display
Team

The Aircraft Histories
and
Current Operation

David Jackson

The Wider View

Acknowledgements

This is my first excursion into authorship and I have found it gratifying that so many people with the relevant knowledge and information were willing to help. They are, in no particular order:

Stewart Ross, Roger Joy, Sqn Ldr Dave Piper RAF, Andy Rake, Dan Griffith, Phil Shaw, Tony Miller, Geoff Burns, Mark Burdett, Bruce Doughty, Chris Cawdron, Dave Bailey, William Sleigh, Richard Paver, Dave Sargent, Dick Teasdale, Hugh Whitmore, Murph Morrison, Barry Jones, Brandon White, Eddie Challoner, Neil Lawes, Ian Kitson, Dave Gearing, Roger Wintle, Arthur Perks.

The Canberra Display Team have also had support from many people and wish to thank many companies within aviation:

The Atlantic Group, Mike Collett, Chris Salter, John Reeve, Mike Day, Annette Bowden, Dave Kingshott, Peter and Frances Gill, Jim Morrow, Martin Baker Aircraft PLC, Quest Inspection, Kidde Graviner, Spies Hecker, CFS Aero Products, Chris Harris DTEO-QinetiQ Boscombe Down, Survival Equipment Services Kemble, NDT Services East Midlands Airport, Basketweb Design Stamford.

And finally to the ladies for putting up with their husbands' magnificent obsession over the years.

The opinions expressed in this publication are those of the author and do not necessarily reflect those of the Canberra Display Team.

David Jackson

Edited and typeset by Tony Miller, Ilton, Somerset

Printed in Great Britain by Stylaprint, Ailsworth, Cambridgeshire

Published and distributed by *The Wider View*, 'Dystlegh', Rod Lane, Ilton, Ilminster, Somerset, TA19 9ET

Dedication

For Barbara, whose idea it was that I should write the book and for the encouragement when I needed it.

Contents

Foreword

The beginning of the twentieth century witnessed the dawn of powered flight, the first of which was achieved on 17th December 1903 when Wilbur and Orville Wright flew their heavier-than-air flying machine. After which there were rapid developments over the following six decades leading to space travel and the spectacular first landing of man on the moon's surface on 21st July 1969 by Neil Armstrong and Edwin Aldrin. In between these two epic events which captured international attention were many other historic achievements.

Such as the first non-stop crossing of any ocean on 14th June 1919 when John Alcock and Arthur Witten-Brown became the first aviators to cross the North Atlantic in a Vickers Vimy, flying from Newfoundland to Ireland, a distance of 1,890 miles. Another such event occurred just over a decade later, on 13th September 1931, when Flight Lieutenant John Boothman flying the Supermarine S6B, captured the third successive Schneider Trophy contest by winning it outright for Britain.

The Schneider Trophy victory occurred at the dawn of a new decade that was to witness the greatest conflict in human history with the outbreak of the Second World War on 3rd September 1939. It was a conflict in which the importance of aircraft as a primary weapon was recognised at the outset. The arms race leading up to and during the war years resulted in Britain's aircraft industry producing some of the finest military aircraft ever built.

As the dark clouds gathered over Europe's political scene the month of January 1933 witnessed two simultaneous events; the first was the appointment of Adolf Hitler as Chancellor of Germany. The second was Rolls Royce's initiative to invest in the future by commencing a design to produce a new generation of aero-engine for the RAF designated the PV-12 (later renamed Merlin). At the same time as Rolls Royce committed its own funds to this project it also gave the Hawker and the Supermarine aircraft companies £5,000 each towards the design of monoplane fighters able to accept this more powerful engine; their efforts culminated in the Hurricane and Spitfire.

In the post-war era at the Rolls Royce airfield at Hucknall, Nottinghamshire, (the same airfield from which the prototype PV-12 engine had commenced its development flying) the company's Chief Test Pilot, Captain Ronald Shepherd, made another of his many firsts. On 15th August 1948 he flew the experimental Lancastrian VM732 which was part-powered by a pair of the company's first prototype axial flow jet engines, the RA2 Avon. The flight was directed at their advanced airworthiness approval for English Electric's new Type A1 aircraft. This flight test programme preceded the Type A1's first flight by nine months, the A1 being the first prototype Canberra VN799 which was flown on the 13th May 1949. Just as the Merlin-powered aircraft of the earlier project remains in RAF service for ceremonial duties so, too, does the Avon-powered Canberra, 50 years after its first flight.

In 1935, a small group of Air Ministry scientists working on the Suffolk coast were undertaking highly secret feasibility experiments to establish the practicability of using reflected radio waves to detect the presence of aircraft. This was in order to provide early warning of any pending attack and was to be the birth of the new science of Radio Direction Finding (RDF), as it was initially designated. It came to be known as Radio-Direction-And Ranging (RADAR) technology that was to transform all future warfare.

The 1935 experiments not only resulted in Britain's coastline being protected by a chain of early warning radar stations by 1940 but, in parallel, the scientists were also applying this technology for radar equipment to be carried in aircraft. This in turn gave birth to a dedicated RAF experimental flying unit; in the pre-war period it was titled the Special Duties Flight. During the war, when the Unit had some 130 aircraft on strength, it was renamed the Telecommunications Flying Unit, a discreet title to arouse as little curiosity as possible. After the war its title was changed again to the Royal Radar Establishment Aircraft Department, when it became the largest operator of Canberra aircraft in the UK. Amongst this fleet of over twenty Canberra aircraft on its flight line were Canberra B Mk.6s WK163, WT327, WT333, XH567 and XH568, all now privately owned in Britain and America.

Britain must be grateful to those dedicated groups, such as the Canberra Display Team, whose members spend long hours of hard work and face associated risks to preserve this country's military aviation heritage for the interest and pleasure of the public. Their particular Canberra aircraft was not standard service issue, but one of a specialist few at the frontiers of military research whose role was fundamental to the effective power of a whole Air Force. In preservation may they continue to prosper.

William Sleigh
Former Chief Engineer
Aircraft Department
Royal Radar Establishment, Pershore

Introduction

The Canberra was the first aircraft I have a clear memory of as a child. The first images I saw were black and white photographs that my father had from his time with 16 Sqn at Laarbruch during the early sixties. I saw my first 'live' Canberra (a 39 Sqn PR7 lone-ranger) whilst we were stationed in Hong Kong at the beginning of the seventies. I never thought at the time that 30 years later I would become involved with one on the national airshow scene. The aircraft itself is one of my all time favourites.

Although the design is now in its sixth decade it is the epitome of early post-war British aviation engineering excellence. The longevity of the type is the stuff of legend; the Royal Air Force still operates a handful in the photographic reconnaissance role. The Canberra enjoyed great export success, too, with the type continuing in service in India and Peru.

Everyone I had cause to speak with during the writing of this book held the aircraft in high regard. During my research I was able to find out more about the early years of the Canberras' operation, especially in relation to WK163. The many hours spent reading through its documentation exploded one or two popular myths about the aeroplane and its activities at Armstrong Siddeley Motors; never being fitted with Sapphire 7s or flying from Filton on short-life Viper work. The documentation also showed how successful (in the case of Napier Ltd. gaining the third and final height record for the aircraft type), and occasionally dangerous, flight testing new technology could sometimes be.

The group's other Canberra, B Mk.6 (mod) XH568 also proved to have an interesting history although I found very little about its early years with the ATDU. Again, reading through its documentation revealed a mass of information and showed that it was a well travelled aircraft, its flights spanning the globe while in use with the Meteorological Research Flight at RAE Farnborough. Later on, alongside WK163, it would prove itself to be a valuable asset in the research and development role as a vehicle for testing the pioneering work that was being undertaken in radar technology at the Royal Radar Establishment Pershore. This work would see both aircraft continuing to fly on defence research projects right up to their eventual retirement in the mid 1990s.

Outside of military operation, W E W Petter's design is still to be found in aviation museums around the world. Other examples are fortunate to be flying in private ownership in Britain, Australia and America. Private operation of the Canberra for display purposes by various groups in the UK began in the early 1990s, the most notable being Classic Aviation Projects Ltd.

Operating under the banner of the Canberra Display Team (CDT) they have managed to operate two Canberras back to back on the airshow circuit since their formation in 1994. The reputation they have today as a first class airshow act has been hard won. With no financial support forthcoming it has meant that individuals within the group have had to finance the entire operation from their own pockets. These individuals are not millionaires by any stretch of the imagination; they are ordinary people who have a desire to succeed in what they do. The early years of display operation were especially hard with almost no financial return to show for the group's efforts.

CDT has been fortunate in other ways, though, in securing the services of a group of highly skilled aircrew and engineers, all of whom give their time and considerable expertise freely. Some members of the group give the impression of almost fanatical dedication to the aircraft. This being all the more noticeable in this day and age, when people have very little free time outside of work and even less again when there is no remuneration involved. One thing I did notice (whether it was working alongside the team during the aircraft servicing or observing the aircrew prior to a display flight) is that they are all consummate professionals. It was never the idea to display the aircraft and make vast amounts of money; the fickle nature of the airshow industry has proved time and again that it cannot be done. The team has only ever had one goal; and that is to make enough financially to cover the operating costs, to ensure that they could fly these classic British aircraft for another season.

Dave Jackson
March 2006

Plate 1 - Graham Hackett and Tony Miller display XH568 at RAF Cosford in 1996.

Mark Burdett collection

Plate 2 - WK163 waits in the afternoon sun at Luton prior to launching to commemorate the 40th anniversary of the Scorpion-assisted record-breaking flight; 28th August 1997.

Author's photograph

Armstrong Siddeley Ltd.
WK163 and the Viper ASVT Trials

At the beginning of the 1950s the British aviation industry utilised the Canberra airframe for testing a whole range of new designs. Armstrong Siddeley Motors Ltd. at Bitteswell, Leicestershire, was no different. Amongst the many different aircraft types being used for development testing by the company's engine division was a small batch of Canberra B Mk.2s. All the company's Canberras were engaged on development work with either the Sapphire or Viper engine programmes. The Sapphire Canberra test airframes had the reputation of being 'hot rods'; the Sapphire Mk.7 engine in particular had a seventy percent increase in power over the Rolls Royce Avon Mk.1 fitted to the standard production examples. At an early stage in development tests at Bitteswell, this airframe and engine combination proved to have startling performance.

Canberra B Mk.2 WD933 (the fifth production aircraft) had been with Armstrong Siddeley Motors (ASM) since April 1951 and had initially been fitted with Sapphire 6 engines, then in early 1952 it was re-engined with the Sapphire 7. The life of this aircraft came to an abrupt and spectacular end on 10th November 1954 when, after an engine relight failed and the other was inadvertently shut down, the aircraft was put down 'wheels up' on the grass adjacent to the main runway at Bitteswell. However, when the aircraft made contact with the runway intersection, it flipped onto its back and continued travelling some distance in that position. ASM chief test pilot Jim Starky and test observer Peter Taylor were fortunate to exit the wreck none the worse for the experience.

Canberra B Mk.2 WV787 arrived at Bitteswell in September 1952 direct from English Electric at Preston and was dedicated to the Sapphire ASSa6R re-heat programme for eventual use in the Gloster Aircraft Company's Javelin all-weather fighter. In January 1955 two more Canberra B2s arrived at Bitteswell. First was WK141, which had been transferred from RAF charge and flown from Aldergrove direct to Bitteswell on the 14th of that month. It was re-engined with Sapphire ASSa7s almost immediately and proceeded to continue the development work that WD933 had done previously.

WK163, built as part of Avro contract No. 6/Acft/5990/CB6(b), arrived on the 28th January direct from Avro's assembly line at Woodford. Armstrong Siddeley were at this time developing the AS Viper series of turbo-jet engines. Development had begun in 1951, the first flight being flown from Bitteswell in November 1952 with the new Viper design fitted into the rear end of Lancaster III SW342. During 1953 the company was developing the Viper 3 for use in the Australian GAF Jindivik high performance target drone.

The engine was type tested at 13,400rpm giving 1,600lbs of thrust. The specification of the design required the drone to reach an altitude of 50,000ft, which disqualified the Viper Lancaster from performing the required test flights.

Not being required for the Sapphire test programme, Canberra WK163 was allocated to the Viper project. On 4th February 1955 Viper 3 engine Serial No.VP1112 was fitted to the aircraft, it being encased in a pod that was fitted to the starboard wing, outboard of the main Avon engine and set at an angle of 2 degrees, 16 inches from the aircraft's datum.

To accommodate the engine mounting brackets under the wing, several 'fingers' on the lower airbrake stem were removed so as not to interfere with their operation when fully extended in the airflow. A new instrument panel was installed at the observer's position containing the main engine controls for the test engine.

Plate 3 - Arriving at Bitteswell in January 1955, the same month as WK163, Canberra B Mk.2 WK141 was put to work on Sapphire engine development.
Author's collection

Plate 4 - June 1955, the general scene on Number 1 site at Bitteswell. From left, Sapphire-powered Hunter F5s WP113 and WP114, Blackburn YB1 WB797, Canberra WK163, Sapphire Lancastrian VM733. Just visible under the fuselage of the Lancastrian is Viper Lancaster III SW342.

Peter Taylor collection

Flight testing was overseen by Peter Aked from Avro Co. Woodford as acting Chief Test Pilot (deputising for Jim Starky), ASM company pilots Jim Bartlam, Harry Rayner and Albert 'Witty' Wittridge would also share the project flying. Ground running of the Viper commenced on the 7th April with no major problems. Some damage was caused to the engine on the 14th April when trapped fuel ignited during a ground run, but fitting a shroud to the jet-pipe clamp joint, along with an external drain, rectified this problem.

Flight testing the Viper commenced on the 16th April with the pilots reporting that the test engine had no significant effect on the aircraft's handling. Further flights saw the Viper being tested at high altitude with shutdown and relight tests being initiated. On the 11th May 1955 Viper serial No.VP1112 was replaced, being time expired after a total of 10 hours and 30 minutes running time.

A second Viper 3, No.VP1113, was installed and, after initial ground running, testing continued much the same as before. The second Viper installation was run until it, too, was time expired after a total of 10 hours. On the 29th June Viper serial No.VP1112 was reinstalled on WK163 after overhaul.

This engine was run for a further 3 hours and 15 minutes on test after which Viper engine development was completed on WK163. In all the aircraft flew a total of 28 development

Plate 5 - ASM Test Observers John Curtiss and Ian Matheson in front of WK163 at Bitteswell.

Peter Taylor collection

flights after which the engine installation and all associated equipment was removed during September 1955. The aircraft was then held in reserve at Bitteswell, only being flown occasionally. During October, various modifications were carried out on the aircraft as part of a fleet-wide programme prior to it being handed over to D. Napier and Son at Luton.

November saw WK163 flying from Bitteswell on post-modification checks with its final flight under ASM charge on the 9th of that month. On the 2nd December, Napier pilot Ken Cartwright collected the aircraft for its flight to Luton and its next phase of engine testing.

Although WK163 was only with ASM for 11 months, the development and systems modifications for the Viper project that were used on the airframe proved that the concept worked. These were later put to good use when the Viper high altitude development programme was re-commenced in 1958 with Sapphire Canberra WK141.

Plate 6 - The Napier Double Scorpion Rocket Motor as fitted to WK163, WT207 and WT208.

Chris Cawdron collection

Napier Ltd.
WK163 and the testing of the Napier Scorpion Rocket Motor

The firm of D. Napier & Sons Ltd. had been part of the English Electric group of companies since the mid-1940s. During the Second World War they had developed the 24-cylinder 3000hp Sabre engine that powered the Hawker Typhoon and Tempest fighters to such good effect. Amidst the ongoing development of rocket weapons around 1950 the interest of the company's Flight Development Establishment (FDE) was focused on the feasibility of rockets being used to enhance the existing performance of aircraft. The alternative use of such thrust generators was as the main power plant for a supersonic, fast-climbing interceptor. The FDE was led by manager Cecil Cowdrey, with Kenneth Greenly as chief engineer. Edward 'Ted' Davies was the FDE's chief designer, and the Rocket Projects division was headed by Alan Fletcher. Rocket development was overseen by Phil Ramsden and flight testing by Duncan Wood. The flight crews involved in the project were led by Napier Chief Test Pilot Mike Randrup and included fellow company pilots Tom Lampitt, Ken Cartwright and Harry Partington. Test observers on the project were Walter Shirley (the FDE's Deputy Chief Engineer) and Duncan Wood.

In pursuit of this defence project, four propulsion systems emerged; besides Napier's Scorpion, there was the de Havilland Co.'s Spectre rocket motor and Armstrong Siddeley's Snarler and Screamer rocket motors. The Napier and de Havilland projects were fuelled by kerosene-HTP whilst ASM's designs were fuelled by liquid oxygen. With the development of the Napier Scorpion series underway for the Ministry of Supply, it was decided that the new rocket motor would be flight tested in a Canberra aircraft, as the design lent itself well to the requirements of the project.

The initial installation in Canberra WK163 comprised a 450 gallon HTP (hydrogen test peroxide) tank. This was cylindrical in shape and approximately 3ft in diameter with hemispherical ends; the tank itself occupied most of the bomb bay. The Scorpion rocket motor was mounted in the rear of the bomb bay with the nozzle exits about one foot forward of the rear bulkhead. Its thrust chambers were inclined at a shallow angle, putting the thrust line close to the aircraft C of G. The cutaway aft of the bomb bay was panelled with stainless steel and the engine was enclosed in a stainless steel cowling. Filling of the HTP tank was through a 'flight refuelling' valve installed on the starboard

Plate 7 - Crewed by Tom Lampitt and Duncan Wood, WK163 lifts off from Farnborough in 1956.

Barry Jones collection

lower fuselage just forward of the bomb bay.

The HTP tank was pressurised with nitrogen from gas bottles installed in the equipment bay behind the cockpit. The tank pressure was initially 10psi, later increased to 12psi, and finally 15psi for the altitude record flights. An HTP jettison pipe ran from the tank to the end of the fuselage internally, except for the last few feet under the tailplane. Kerosene was supplied to the rocket engine from the aircraft fuel system at normal boost pump pressure.

The first version of the Scorpion to fly was configured like a twin thrust chamber engine, however only one thrust chamber was operative. The single Scorpion engine, designated NScS 1-1 with serial numbers starting at 101, completed a type test programme and flight-testing was started in the spring of 1956, with the aircraft being demonstrated at the Paris airshow in May that year.

This first engine was removed from the aircraft in June 1956 after completing about thirty minutes running without any significant problems. The double Scorpion engine was by now ready for flight-testing, having completed a two-hour type test consisting of primarily three minute runs with typically one hour cool down periods in between. These three minute firings were usually cycled from full thrust to half thrust by switching the second thrust unit on and off in a couple of simple sequences. The early double Scorpions were coded NScD 1-1, with serial numbers starting at 201, and after being extensively tested on a rig which utilised the rear fuselage of prototype Canberra VX165 were first flown in June 1956.

The control panel at the observer's station in WK163 was modified with instruments and switches for propellant isolation valves, tank pressurisation, HTP jettison, instrument camera and the two engine starters fitted with guard plates. The engine starters were wired in series with another pair at the pilot's position. The pilot also had a master switch that isolated the rocket engine controls. A second panel in front of the flight observer showed basic flight instruments, propellant feed, start system, pump delivery, combustion chamber pressures, coolant outlet, engine bay temperatures, turbine overspeed and fuel valve indicator lights.

The aircraft was flown by Napier pilots Ken Cartwright, Harry Partington and Tom Lampitt. These flight tests covered endurance running, flame spread, cold starting at altitude, climb performance and a number of demonstration flights. There were no major problems with the rocket motor, with only a few minor component failures before the first Double Scorpion completed one hour's flight running time. It was found that the rocket exhaust flame expanded at 40,000ft with the original shallow angle engine installation.

The cold starting set out to simulate a half hour patrol at 40,000ft which soon demonstrated that engine bay temperatures fell below 0°C at which starting became unreliable. This was not unexpected, as trials had been carried out with a ground rig in Canada during the winter of

1956. Engine-bay heating was installed using main engine compressor air, and adequate bay temperatures for reliable starting were quickly established.

The climb performance was measured on several occasions during climbs between 10,000 and 40,000ft. The aircraft was demonstrated at the Farnborough show in 1957 with engine No.203 installed. By mid-1957 the 300 series engine had passed its type test; the major changes were reconfiguration to suit the intended P1 fighter installation. The thrust chambers were mounted at a steeper angle and inclined outwards, the engine structure was changed from a separate sub-frame carrying the thrust chambers to mountings cast integral with the chamber casing. The turbine starting system was also changed from a nitrogen pressurised spherical tank to an electrical motor driven pump to provide the internal HTP feed to the turbine steam generator. To match the new engine configuration the installation in WK163 was changed, moving the engine forward about three feet so that the thrust line still passed through the aircraft's C of G.

Associated changes were made to the bomb bay doors, rocket engine bay shielding and the HTP tank (which was shortened, reducing its capacity to about 350 gallons). The new installation was ground tested on 5th June 1957 and flight-testing was recommenced. The aircraft was flown to Idris airfield (Castel Benito) Libya for two weeks of hot weather trials in the last half of June 1957. No problems were encountered in about a dozen test flights, with Ken Cartwright and Tom Lampitt piloting and Walter Shirley and Duncan Wood as flight observers. Perhaps the most notable occurrence was that for the first two days it was hotter in London than at Idris!

Prior to the altitude record attempts, test firings were carried out at altitudes up to 45,000ft to establish the exhaust plume boundary with the new installation. In preparation for the altitude record, Randrup, Shirley, Cartwright and Wood were fitted out with pressure suits and the aircraft oxygen system was modified to match.

Three flights were made in establishing the altitude record; the first attempt on the 27th August 1957 did not exceed the previous record by sufficient margin. The second attempt (the first flight on the 28th Aug) was high enough but the sealed barograph malfunctioned so a third run was made the same day. At the time it was thought the second flight reached 73,000ft but handling problems were experienced at the top of the climb and on the final attempt the aircraft did not go quite so high. It was initially thought to be 72,000ft, however the final certified altitude was 73,310ft. WK163 was flown as light as possible for these flights, somewhere around 26-27,000lbs.

The general flight plan for these record climbs was to climb to about 45,000ft before starting the rocket motor. With a rate of climb in the region of about 9,000ft per minute the 70,000ft mark was reached in about three minutes. On the advice of Rolls Royce the Avons were set

Plate 8 - A copy of a 1957 photograph showing Napier staff applying the Scorpion emblem to the nose of WK163.

Author's collection

at a climb-power setting throughout and not altered while at extreme altitudes, to minimise the chances of flame-out.

The Scorpion insignia and altitude record data was painted on the aircraft in time for the Farnborough show. At the 1957 show the aircraft was flown every day by Tom Lampitt and Duncan Wood without any problems. After Farnborough, flight-testing continued with quite a number of demonstration flights. On one occasion during flight-testing attempts were made to photograph the exhaust plume, as the shock pattern expanded considerably at altitude (40,000ft and upward). For these tests a de Havilland Sea Venom was used as a camera platform. The crew of WK163 reported on one occasion that they sailed passed the Venom with the Avons throttled back and airbrakes out at 0.82Mach!

By this time the underside of the rear fuselage was painted with black acid-resistant paint. This area was also affected by acoustic vibration from the rocket engine and at one major inspection WK163 had some fifty or more rivets replaced on the underside of the fuselage. This was a problem that would occur on several occasions during the test programme. As a result of the altitude record publicity, Bomber Command commissioned Napier to fit Scorpion installations to two 76 Sqn Canberra B Mk.6s, WT207 and WT208. These aircraft were to be used for high altitude air sampling in the Grapple nuclear tests, and were required for operations by March 1958.

The installation in WT208 was completed and ground run on 1st February. Thereafter the aircraft was flown by a 76 Sqn crew practising their operational flight plan. This required a Scorpion climb from 45,000ft to 60,000ft followed by a slow decent to 56,000ft, then restarting the Scorpion to climb back to 60,00ft to achieve a maximum sampling time in this height bracket. The sampling equipment for these flights was housed in specially made wing tip tanks, which had been test flown on WK163 several

months previously. After several flights the rocket engine was sealed off and the aircraft flown out to Christmas Island.

It was never used for its intended purpose due to the fact that sister aircraft WT207 had exploded in mid-air while proof testing a Scorpion unit. Needless to say WT208 was not used operationally and it was converted back to bomber configuration upon its return to Britain in June of 1958. WT207 disintegrated following an explosion in the Scorpion engine bay when a restart was being carried out at 56,000ft on the 9th April 1958. Most of the engine was recovered. The No.2 combustion unit was separated from the rest and its head end and kerosene valve was never found. It was evident that there had been an explosion at the forward end of this chamber, since the catalyst pack was pushed hard down to the burner assembly.

The pilot's report described an unusual rumbling noise and fire warning before the explosion. This suggested a failure had occurred at the head of No.2 chamber at/or before the second start resulting in an accumulation of propellants in the bomb bay which subsequently ignited.

Several test firings with an engine incorporating suspected defects such as a porous chamber casting and faulty sealing rings did not reproduce the failure, and the exact cause was not immediately established. However, late in 1958 a chamber casting did fail on start up, despite rigorous manufacturing inspection and pressure testing procedures. As a result a design change from aluminium to stainless steel casings was put in hand in early 1959. The Scorpion programme was cancelled in 1959's Government Defence White Paper, no longer being considered necessary as a booster unit for the new P1 (Lightning) fighter.

It is interesting to note that, reading the Form F700 that was in use at the time of the height record, there is no mention of the achievement in the after-flight certificate. Just another day at the office! Its job done at Napier, WK163 was transferred to RRE fleet holdings on the 30th April 1959.

Bombs and Mines
XH568 at the Air Torpedo Development Unit

Canberra B Mk.6 XH568 was built by English Electric Preston as part of contract No 6/Acft/11313/CB6(b). The aircraft joined the Air Torpedo Development Unit (ATDU) at Gosport, Hampshire, straight from the manufacturers on the 1st March 1955. Along with two other aircraft, Canberra B Mk.6 XH567 and B Mk.22 WH661, it was used in flight trials for retarded airborne delivery of the Mk.12 aerial mine. This weapon was torpedo-like in shape with a detachable tail section, and deployed a small parachute after release to slow down the rate of descent to its target area. The only noticeable change to these aircraft was the addition of a camera pod fitted to the underside of each wing tip, these being secured to the wing in the same manner as the standard tip tanks. The cameras recorded the weapon release from the aircraft. The aircraft's bomb bay housed a third camera and modified bomb beam, to which the mines were attached.

The trials were conducted from Gosport and West Freugh and generally testing went according to plan, although the occasional problem did occur. One such occurrence happened on the 28th November 1957 when the nose cone on one of two Mk.12 mines being carried by XH568 became detached. The errant nose cone caused severe damage to the rear of both bomb doors, the port side bomb bay wall and rear bulkhead before falling away from the aircraft. The damage was subsequently repaired and XH568 continued to fly various anti-shipping weapon trials with the ATDU until the 12th December 1958 when it was transferred to the RAE Farnborough, joining the air assets of the Meteorological Research Flight (MRF).

XH568 at the RAE
Travelling the World with Flook

After arrival at Farnborough, XH568 underewent major servicing between 16th December 1958 and 10th August 1959, prior to starting its flying duties with the Meteorological Research Flight. On 11th January 1960, XH568 was flying its first overseas trip to El Adem in Libya, the flight from Farnborough taking around 3hrs 30mins. By the end of the month the aircraft was back at the RAE, being back in the hangar by the 26th for further modification under ASI/STR2/60.

At the end of April 1960 the Canberra emerged from the workshops looking somewhat different; for its new role with the MRF Structures department it had been fitted with a 12ft nose probe in place of the standard Perspex nose cone. This probe contained pressure-sensing apparatus, which transferred all collected data to an instrumentation crate that was housed in the bomb bay. The aircraft was also part painted in a motley scheme of white, Day-Glo orange and silver!

In the early 1960s the RAE was conducting research into gust measurement of air turbulence associated with jet streams. The data collected on these flights would later be used in selecting suitable high altitude air lanes for the new type of long-range airliners then under design. Later, this research would extend to thunderstorm penetration (structures scientist Anne Burns [1] headed the overall research project). To get the required data the project determined that flights were to be made in parts of the world where there was a constant high level jet stream in place, a task that would take XH568 all over the world looking for weather systems. Several early sorties were flown from Luqa in Malta and El Adem in Libya, the Middle East having favourable high-pressure regions. These flights were flown between 30,000 and 40,000ft.

In August 1961 XH568 was back in the workshop at Farnborough, where further modifications and installations were carried out under ASI/STR16/61. This work entailed fitting the aircraft with a new 15ft nose probe and covering the leading edge of both wings, tail fin and engine intakes with plastic material to prevent erosion during extreme weather flights. The aircraft's engine controls were also altered so as to have continuous re-light in operation. Finally the Canberra was repainted white overall with large areas of high visibility arctic red on both wings as well as the nose and tail sections.

During February 1962 the aircraft was back flying research sorties. On the 4th April 1962 XH568 received some damage from a lightning strike to the nose probe while flying through thunderstorms off the south coast of France. The aircraft diverted to Hyeres as a precaution. It was found that the tip of the nose probe had taken the full load of the charge and showed burn damage to that effect. The tip of the starboard elevator was also damaged where the strike had discharged itself. Repairs were put in hand to enable the Canberra to get back to Farnborough. Once there it was subject to a complete check of the airframe and all systems for any further damage.

The aircraft flew to Australia in May 1963 staging through Cyprus, Aden, Gan and Singapore before arriving

Plate 9 - XH568 at Tinker AFB in June 1966. Note the Flook and kangaroo 'zaps' on the tail, a legacy from the Australian detachment of the previous year.
Barry Jones collection

Plate 10 - XH568 photographed at Llanbedr in 1961.

Author's collection

at Woomera in South Australia. During the next five months the aircraft operated between Woomera and Townsville in Queensland. The pilot of XH568 for the trip was Murph Morrison who remembered the trials:

"For the jet stream trials in Australia the starboard engine of the aircraft was fitted with a smoke generator. When switched on it injected diesel into the jet pipe causing a smoke trail; we also had a 150-gallon Derv tank fitted at the rear of the bomb bay, which fed the generator. The smoke trail would make it possible to visually plot the air turbulence and also photograph it with the aircraft's on-board cameras, hopefully to tie up with the recording traces from the instrumentation pack once downloaded after the sortie."

During the aircraft's time in Australia it acquired the nickname 'Flook' after the cartoon character that was popular on television at the time. It also received the appropriate Flook and Kangaroo zaps to its tail!

After completing project trials in Australia, XH568 flew back to the UK via the Cocos Islands, Gan, and Aden spending a week based at Entebbe in Uganda and flying through heavy tropical thunderstorms. By the end of September XH568 was back at Farnborough. On the 12th December 1963 the aircraft was taken out of service so that a major servicing could take place, the airframe having

flown a total of 1,027 hrs. With major serving complete in March 1964, XH568 was then test flown prior to going back into the workshops for more installation work to be carried out. This work would see the Canberra out of service until November of that year.

1965 duly arrived and XH568 would be off on its travels again with a trip to the USA in May that year. The aircraft would be based at Tinker Air Force Base (AFB) Oklahoma, again on gust research. The trip staged through Lossiemouth, Keflavik, Sondrestrom, Goose Bay, Loring, Stewart and Wright Patterson AFBs before arrival at Tinker. The American detachment was a short one, as the aircraft was back in the UK by the middle of July. A minor servicing followed in October 1965, with the aircraft returning to duty in March 1966. The next 12 months would see various 'local' trips to such destinations as Bodo, Wildenrath, Florennes, Ramstein, Cyprus and Gibraltar. In June 1967 XH568 was in the workshops to have all MRF installations removed prior to being transferred to the RRE at Pershore; the Canberra was flown to its new home on the 28th December 1967.

[1] *Anne Burns had been part of the RAE structures team involved with successfully investigating the cause of airframe failure that had seen the loss of two de Havilland Comet airliners during the early 1950s.*

In Ministry of Defence Service

The Origins of Airborne Radar

The use of the Canberra aircraft as an airborne trials platform for radar systems dates from 1951 when the third prototype, VN828, was allocated to the RAF Telecommunications Flying Unit (TFU) at Defford, Worcestershire. The flight trials organisation of the then highly classified Telecommunications Research Establishment (TRE) was originally created by the Air Ministry in 1936 as the Bawdsey Research Station on the Suffolk coast. Its aim was to explore, develop and construct the successful Chain Home (CH) early warning and integrated fighter defence management system.

At that time, before the title *Radar* was introduced, this facility was referred to as Radio Direction Finding (RDF). In parallel with the development of the CH system for air defence, the future application of this new science as an airborne aid to accurately identify targets, navigate in any state of visibility, use for reconnaissance and for any other purposes was also being explored by the Bawdsey scientists. These first airborne experiments were being undertaken by a newly-created small dedicated Special Duties Flight (SDF). Initially hosted by Aircraft and Armaments Experimental Establishment (A&AEE) conveniently located at Martlesham Heath airfield, the Flight was hurriedly relocated to Boscombe Down airfield on outbreak of war. After three temporary moves, the SDF was, in August 1942, finally allocated the newly constructed airfield at Defford in continued support of the parent TRE, which had been relocated for reasons of high national security to Malvern, Worcestershire. By this stage the former SDF had considerably expanded, being titled the RAF TFU and awarded its own Unit crest. Its complement of 2,000 personnel also operated 130 aircraft, as well as handling many others.

The new science of airborne radar now attracted the major share of the Government's R&D funding on which the whole future capability of military aviation was to depend. Unlike other areas of aeronautical research, scientists engaged in the research into radar systems had no affinity with aeronautical engineering; their task was only to devise electronic equipment for fitting to aircraft and to bridge this critical void.

In early 1939 the Air Ministry had a nucleus of aeronautical engineers drafted from the Radio Department of the Royal Aircraft Establishment, Farnborough (RAE), to the Bawdsey Research Station. In this team of young specialists was the designer David K Henderson, later to be responsible for all aircraft design modification for the installation of radar systems. Also in the team was Derek

H Mosely, likewise undertaking the workshop fitting and hangar installation of experimental hardware. Both were to serve their entire careers within this specialist organisation that covered the period when the unit handled over 46 Canberra aircraft.

By the mid 1960s it was operating a total of 22 aircraft of this type on its flight lines, thus becoming the largest operator of Canberra aircraft in the UK. David Henderson, whose team handled over 100 types involving more than 800 aircraft on the unit, was an experienced engineer of considerable foresight and initiative. During the post-war years, as the unit's Chief Engineer with overall technical responsibility, he was exclusively responsible for the selection of future radar trials aircraft and also for implementing their structural modifications. In some cases this work was very extensive, for which he had built up appropriate workshop resources over many years to become an autonomous engineering authority.

The dawn of the Radar fleet Canberra era

The introduction of the Canberra aircraft during the dawn of the jet age in the early 1950s attracted Henderson's attention as it had considerable potential as an airborne trials platform for the flight development of future generations of British military radar. With an altitude capability of up to 50,000ft, speed up to 450knots/530mph and range of 1,800 miles, its maximum payload for experimental equipment was 10,000lbs. The strong, easily accessible airframe structure offered both internal space and external attachments with unlimited opportunities. A further significant technical attraction was the provision in each inboard wing of an engine driven auxiliary gearbox each fitted with a 6kW generator and a hydraulic pump.

The auxiliary drive gear boxes were made by the RoTol Company of Gloucester, a jointly owned subsidiary company founded in May 1937 by Rolls-Royce and the Bristol Aero Engine Company to meet both firms' needs for propellers and auxiliary drive equipment. The gearboxes were unique in themselves as, with technical foresight, the basic design provisioned five attachment faces per gearbox to which a future type of hydraulic or electrical service could be attached. Thus, in addition to the two faces already utilised for the Canberra's basic needs, there remained a further three 'vacant' faces for additional electrical power for which the respective strengths of Avon engine output gears and gear box drive shafts were more than adequate.

Thus there was an immense future potential for the whole concept which was to be exploited to the full by the

Radar Establishment's aircraft engineers. Ultimately, in addition to the aircraft's basic needs of 6kW per gear box, installations were able to accommodate up to 22kVA power. This dedicated fleet based at Pershore also served Britain's main radar contractors sponsored by the MoD through the Royal Radar Establishment (RRE) amongst whom were EMI, Marconi, Ferranti and others. Some of these large companies holding major contracts had out-station facilities on the airfield.

Transfer to Pershore in 1957

The changing defence requirements of the mid 1950s heralded the arrival of new types of jet aircraft and with it the need for longer runways with higher load carrying capabilities to facilitate operation up to V-bomber class aircraft. The wartime airfield of Defford had unsuitable flight path approaches for jet aircraft to the main runways of only 2,000 yards. Their surfaces being under-strength for future requirements resulted in the Unit being relocated in 1957 to the former wartime airfield at nearby Pershore. In addition to the RRE operating V-bombers, the airfield also served as an operational dispersal for the RAF Bomber Command's V-Force aircraft of that time. New modern design offices, structural test facilities and improved workshop resources, including engineering testing and science laboratories, were provided.

It was at Pershore that most of the major structural modifications were undertaken on the Canberra fleet and where Henderson set up Canberra partial reconditioning facilities. Referred to as the 'PRC' line, it also accepted other MoD R&D fleet Canberra aircraft within RRE's programme planning. Prior to the transfer to Pershore the parent establishment had been re-titled the Royal Radar Establishment. With the airfield having been 'civilianised' after the war, many former RAF maintenance personnel of the former TFU stayed with the organisation which, in turn, was re-titled the RRE Aircraft Department. The Unit's integral flying wing of RAF aircrew (the only remaining Air Force presence) was re-named the Radar Research Flying Unit (RRFU), including the re-issue of a revised Service crest. It was this latter title that became synonymous with the Canberra aircrew of that era.

The Canberra soon became the establishment's main laboratory aircraft amongst the various other types operated. Unlike most other aircraft of the time, English Electric had based its design on the 'split assembly' technique, in which the finished aircraft was assembled from already completed major airframe components having very accurately matched interface frames. This enabled the eventual Mark number of the finished aircraft to be dictated at the assembly stage by the structures selected, ie. the types of front (cabin) fuselage structures unique to future role and the choice of either of two distinct types of wings, the latter also being unique to the two types of Avon engines available. In this viable 'mix-and-match' arrangement an aircraft with a standard three-crew cabin for the bomber role was a straight B Mk.2 with 6,500lbs thrust Avon Mk.101 engines and associated (non fuel) 'dry' wings. Thus, by changing these wings for the upgraded type each incorporating a 450-gallon integral fuel tank and the 7,500lbs thrust Avon Mk.109 engines the

Plate 11 - WK163 at Pershore in 1970. Note the cutout in the bomb bay to accommodate the Winkfield satellite programme trials installation.

Mark Burdett collection

aircraft then became a straight B Mk.6.

Similarly, if a B(I) Mk.8 airframe (as assembled by EE with the upgraded wings incorporating the Avon Mk.109 engines) had its forward Interdictor fuselage exchanged for a three crew bomber forward fuselage it automatically became a standard B Mk.6 variant.

The two photographic variants, the PR Mks.3 and 7 with the integrally built centre and rear fuselages, again differed only by the standard of wings fitted, the former with Avon Mk.101 and the latter with Avon Mk.109 engines. The only odd variant was the Short PR Mk.9 with each wing tip extended by 18 inches and engine mounts for the 10,000lbs thrust Avon Mk.206 engines for high altitude operation.

The 'split assembly' construction offered any operator the opportunity to change the Mark number of Canberra aircraft with no legacy of its previous build standard. There were no half & half numbers such as a B Mk.2/6 or B(I) Mk.8/6 from the foregoing examples. In practice such a need never arose in mainstream RAF service and appears unique to RRE Aircraft Department's requirements.

(Above) Plate 12 - Part of a Canberra self-assembly kit! The forward fuselage of WK135 during conversion to long-nose configuration prior to being fitted to WT333 at Pershore in 1974.

(Below) Plate 13 - The cutouts in the bomb doors and the pod fixed in the bomb bay of WT333 shows the extent of the modification work that could be undertaken on a trials aircraft to meet the needs of the scientists.

Both from the author's collection

Plate 14 - XH568 acquires an extended forward fuselage to join the ranks of the long-nose fleet; Pershore 1970.
Author's collection

The objective behind Henderson's engineering policy of interchanging front fuselages was one of ensuring the availability on the flight line of a fully provisioned laboratory aircraft well in advance of the predicted commencement date of the flight trials for any major scientific programme.

In any specific case where an aircraft's availability to meet the required date of the first project flight could be achieved more quickly by fitting a fuselage structure already converted to the ultimate standard on another aircraft of lower priority, then a change of front fuselage was planned and implemented. Under this engineering policy no defence project was ever delayed by the non-availability of an aircraft.

That policy was augmented by the parallel support of TRE/RRE resident Scientific Superintendent on the airfield, Ralph E Mills. He was a long-standing colleague of Henderson, had been a founder member of both the Air Ministry research station at Bawdsey in 1936 and the original Special Duties Flight and had accumulated many hundreds of experimental flying hours during and immediately after the war years.

Had such an in-house aeronautical engineering facility not existed it would have necessitated the radar scientific staff, who by background had no connection with or technical interests in aeronautical matters, to contract out their requirements to the aircraft industry. That would have required the raising of a work specification and supporting contract, the creation of which would almost certainly have seriously inhibited progress. Any time scale inhibition was instantly circumvented by having a dedicated in-house aircraft structural fabrication resource.

The flying unit's respective aeronautical, mechanical and electrical design offices not only interpreted scientific requirement, but also updated changes into hardware with the parallel activity of the workshops 'cutting metal' from priority issue drawings raised in advance of others.

If aircrew stations were the subject of redesign, the RAF OC Flying was invited to attend on-site design meetings and inspect subsequent mock-up displays to seek his agreement with regard to ejection seat clearances and other relevant safety matters.

Airfield engineering management appraisals established that this approach to major radar installations in aircraft by a small, highly motivated and cohesive organisation, working to its own comprehensive planning schedules (Critical Path Networks), showed savings of approximately 40% in cost and time when compared with the essential administrative procedures necessary had the work been contracted out to industry. This direct engineering approach, having been developed as standard practice by the Unit through necessity during the Second World War, continued during the Canberra era under the same management team irrespective of work clearance elsewhere in the MoD. David Henderson's post war policy was that all engineering modifications undertaken by RRE Aircraft Department had to be certified to the same standards as those required from the aerospace industry under the Air Form 100C 'Certificate of Design for Special Installation in Aircraft' and the Form RD(A) 13 'Design Certificate for Flight Trials' certificates, and those of the Civil Aviation Authority on appropriate aircraft.

Whilst this regime was still in place, the independent RAF Directorate of Flight Safety, in its 1969 review of flight safety of British military aircraft operation, reported that, although the RAF had achieved a higher standard of safety compared with the Government's research airfields, it singled out RRE Pershore as the airfield having achieved the highest flight safety standard of all in the UK. This was attributed to the standard of facilities on the unit and a highly experienced, unchanging work force which, the report added, was well above average age of that on any Air Force unit.

The unit's aircrew comprised both RAF and RN Fleet Air Arm personnel; the latter for radar trials involving naval aircraft. Both served the normal service tours lasting between two and three years. The aircrews, other than flying sorties to meet these ongoing scientific requirements, had no direct involvement in radar design matters, although aircrew navigators inherently had more of a primary interest in the airborne use of certain systems.

During the unit's 25 years of Canberra operation preceding the closure of Pershore it experienced two

looking radar devices such as target acquisition and terrain avoidance systems, David Henderson decided that a suitable modification to the front fuselage of an aircraft to accommodate all envisaged long-term research would be required.

With the new generations of advanced radar systems significantly benefitting from the transmitter and receiver units being as near as possible to the radar aerial head, in preference to being located in the bomb bay with associated cabling, Henderson envisaged providing such a facility in an extended Canberra front fuselage. The original structural modifications to a Canberra forward fuselage had been carried out on B Mk.6 WH945 in 1957 prior to the TRE moving to new premises at Pershore. This work became the design basis for any future conversions.

Initial preparation involved removal of the aircraft's original front nose fairing forward of fuselage Frame No.1 complete with the bomb aimer's acrylic window, all of which formed the original front compartment. The exposed area was then blanked with a reinforced diaphragm to form the cabin's forward pressure bulkhead.

The new extension built forward of the Frame No.1 bulkhead comprised two separate structures; a fixed cylindrical fuselage of 4ft diameter and 3.4ft long for the equipment compartment (referred to as a monocoque) and the removable radome covering the radar scanner. The rear of the monocoque structure was permanently attached to Frame No.1, with its forward frame being a load-bearing radial casting incorporating the scanner unit attachment points. The whole profile was machined to precise dimensions to form a mating spigot to accept a second annular casting forming the root attachment of the radome. The latter two castings were held firmly together by a manacle clamp, this whole design eliminating stress areas around the periphery of this strong structure.

The radome on any aircraft has to meet nominal flight strength requirements and, as a dielectric structure, it also has to be constructed to very close tolerances dictated by the intended radar frequency band. The radome itself was fabricated with external and internal strong solid laminates, each built-up with many layers of resin impregnated glass cloth, the two laminates being separated

losses; the first tragedy being Canberra B Mk.2 WF892 on 23rd October 1953 when both engines ingested a flock of birds during take-off from Exeter killing the crew. This tragedy was followed four years later when another B2, WK129, failed to return to base on 9th December 1957 from a sortie in the northwest. Its wreckage was later located 3,000 feet up on the Carnedd Lewellyn mountain in north Wales, both crew having been killed. The cause was attributed to engine failure due to severe icing on the inlet guide vanes of the Mk.1 Avon engines.

The long-nose variant

The arrival of the first Canberra aircraft at the Telecommunications Research Establishment Defford in 1951 to support the continuing advancement of radar science was, unknowingly at the time, to herald a new era of aircraft versatility. During the Second World War, the Air Ministry could call on British aviation manufacturers to supply them with as many aircraft that they might need for their various research and development programmes. In the post-war years, however, there were considerably fewer aircraft and the necessity arose to adapt any single aircraft to support as many projects as practical.

The mid to late 1950s was also a period committed to the research and development of homing sensors for guided weapons (GW). The TRE/RRE was the responsible design authority for the complete guidance systems for the various types, which included the Bloodhound and Thunderbird weapons. Thus all GW guidance systems originating from either the laboratories of the Establishment, or those of its contractors, were flight developed by the Aircraft Department.

To achieve the aim of versatile airframes, and to meet the continuing requirement for research into forward

Plate 16 - Two of the long-nose variants, WH660 and WG789, carry out a pairs take-off from Pershore in the mid-1960s.
Chris Cawdron collection

by, and bonded to, a central core of hard plastic foam, the whole forming a very strong sandwich construction. In the case of the Canberra radomes they had a third central laminate forming a double sandwich. Each respective layer when finished was machined to an accuracy of 0.010in (0.25 mm), the final thickness of the finished radome for the aircraft being 0.560in (15mm). The structure then received a 0.010in thick protective coat of neoprene, so this structure, on which an aircraft's operational capability depended, was far from being a simple plastic cowling on the front of a fuselage!

The grounding time to convert any Canberra to meet long-nose build standard was dictated by the work involved on the front fuselage extension which, in addition to the strip out of the whole cabin area and associated refurbishing, could take between nine months and a year. Thus as all these primary fuselage structures were assembled on a 'mix and match' philosophy, affording the opportunity to modify any suitable front fuselage in advance of withdrawing the intended aircraft from other project work until the exchange dates were forecast by the long-term planning programme.

Adaptable Canberra crew station design

Flying trials in support of the RRE had always demanded reasonably accurate position fixing aids to be installed in all aircraft, to give flexible operation over the whole of the United Kingdom air space. The point-source aids using various direction finding and distance measuring techniques, such as ADF (Automatic Direction Finding), VOR (VHF Omni Directional aid) and TACAN (Tactical Air Navigation), were too confining. The navigation aids of radar fleet aircraft were upgraded in the

1950s with the introduction of the Gee Mk.3 pulsed VHF hyperbolic system and the Green Satin, or Blue Silk, Doppler radar. The latter systems enabled crews to fly tracks with an accurate measurement of ground speed. The Doppler equipment's inherent capability to measure along and across track velocities was also used to feed this information to a suitable computer. Together with that of heading information from the aircraft's gyromagnetic compass, this information was essential to some experimental radar systems under development. These navigation facilities were further updated in the mid 1960s, in advance of the planned phasing out of the Gee pulse system, with the new continuous wave Decca Mk.1 (Air) navigation radar towards the end of that decade.

These improvements introduced the lightweight package comprising the Decca Mk.19, Doppler 72 systems and the associated Decca Area Navigation Airborne Computer (DANAC). This had a direct digitised read-out of positional information in place of the earlier space consuming dial presentations, which in turn considerably reduced the navigator's workload.

In the case of unit Canberra aircraft, Henderson decided to exploit this considerable saving in equipment space in the relatively restricted area of the two rear crew stations. This was done by a redesign, involving swapping the navigator's position from the port (left) side behind the pilot, with the bomb aimer's position on the starboard (right). The original front fuselage on Canberra WK163 (now part of WT327) was stripped out of the area concerned, to enable the Design Office to install the temporary mock-up of the envisaged change. The changeover meant that space was made available which was formerly occupied by the redundant and more bulky navigation equipment. This was now used for the installation of the radar observer's displays. The compact digital presentation of the new generation navigation system was easily accommodated on the starboard side. All these changes were stressed to meet the +25g crash case.

Incorporated in these cabin changes was the replacement of the standard rear pressure bulkhead connector panel with a larger type panel to cater for all foreseeable future requirements. This meant having more cable sockets available for connecting system components to either side of the pressure bulkhead.

The other feature included in these changes was the redesign of the aircraft's electrical inverter system to provide alternating current (AC) for the aircraft's instrument and navigation systems from the direct current (DC) fed from the main generators. The changes involved providing this AC power requirement from newly introduced static inverters while the original rotary inverters were retained to supply AC power to the experimental radar systems. This redesign also incorporated an automatic override on-line switch should emergency backup power be needed to supply the aircraft services AC system from the original rotary inverters. The changes also embraced the upgrading of each aircraft's electrical cabling for both aircraft primary services and the requirements of scientific installations. The latter case provided for basic R&D requirements but with extra bulkhead connectors should the need arise for additional supplementary supplies. All cable looms were made in a dedicated cable shop, where connectors were fitted; the cable looms were then tested and certified.

The closure of RRE Aircraft Department

By the late 1960s David Henderson's health necessitated medical absence, so his deputy William H Sleigh became acting Chief Engineer. The appointment was made permanent on Henderson's eventual retirement in 1970, just prior to the Government's rationalisation of the UK defence establishments announced in 1972. The announcement included the closure of the RRE Aircraft Department, Pershore, by 1976 and the transfer of its engineering resources to the Royal Aircraft Establishment (RAE) Bedford. New facilities were to be built there, including design offices and the refurbishment of other essential accommodation.

Prior to the implementation of this amalgamation, a specially appointed Airfleet Management Committee was created at the RAE Farnborough to support the integration. The Committee's final report included an assessment reviewing the depth of structural modifications carried out on aircraft by the various research airfields, in which it concluded that the RRE Aircraft Department had been undertaking the highest percentage of aircraft modification work outside the aircraft industry. In this context, directed

at savings in project cost and time, the final closure of the RRE Aircraft Department's workshops was deferred until the end of 1977. This was brought about by a very late MoD requirement made in that final year for it to modify a new Buccaneer aircraft to incorporate the first prototype front structure and associated radome for the future Tornado F3 Air Defence Variant. The requirement also included approval of this new type's future radar system, the prototype of which had already been developed at Pershore in Canberra WH953. This last commitment to modify Buccaneer Mk.S2B XX897 was achieved under Derek Moseley, who met the required completion date after which he finally retired.

At the time of the closure of Pershore the RAF RRFU was disbanded. Amongst the remaining fleet of nineteen aircraft transferred to the RAE Bedford were the nine surviving Canberras whose structural standards were to remain unaltered until their eventual withdrawal and disposal. Pershore's Chief Engineer transferred to Bedford to become the Aircraft Installations Manager. The remaining staff of the unit's mechanical and electrical design offices included a few other technical staff, all of whom became part of the RAE Aircraft Department. Their departure from Worcestershire thus ended exactly 40 years of aircraft being an integral part of the Radar Establishment's dedicated aviation resource.

Preserved Canberra radar research aircraft

The five privately owned Canberra aircraft of the former RRE Aircraft Department Pershore remained dedicated to the research and proving of many applications of radar science for their remaining years with the Ministry of Defence. They are WK163, WT327, WT333, XH567 and XH568 all of which were reconditioned by the RRE and brought to the B Mk.6 build standard irrespective of their original mark number at the time of manufacture, two being extensively modified with extended fuselages. The individual backgrounds of complex aircraft, which in some cases involved their project flying having overlapping involvement with other types of aircraft, are more readily understood if considered on an aircraft by aircraft basis in calendar order of events rather than numerical order. Details of the three airframes acquired by Classic Aviation Projects are dealt with here, more details of the remainder are contained in *Surviving Airworthy Canberras*, page 39.

WK163, WT333 and XH568

Canberra B Mk.6 XH568 was allocated to Pershore on 28th December 1967 from the Meterological Research Flight, it being a further airframe which met the unit's long-term standardisation requirements for Avon 109 engines and wings. Although the aircraft was intended for use in GW homing head research, the prime reason for its

Plate 17 - WT333 in Quebec during the LRCS trial in 1990. Note the modifications to the radome.

Author's collection

modification was to be available as a dormant backup for Canberra B Mk.6 WH953, which was dedicated to the development of new high priority CW radar technology for the future Tornado ADV F3.

The Installation Workshop started work by converting the front fuselage (No.71105 removed from the unit's redundant Canberra B Mk.2 WG788) to long-nose standard for fitting to XH568 in 1969. This involved the manufacture of a new monocoque, with a slightly repositioned equipment access door, and associated radome. The former WG788 front fuselage, after structural modification and recondition, was passed to the second line servicing PRC line for assembly to the fuselage of XH568. When the refurbishment was completed in late 1970 it became the primary aircraft in the development of the guidance system for the helicopter launched anti-ship weapon called Sea Skua, supported by Canberra B Mk.2 WG789. This aircraft was the carrier for the development of a guidance system for the air-launched anti-ship weapon, later designated Sea Eagle, for which XH568 in turn acted in support. XH568 was transferred to the Royal Aircraft Establishment (RAE) Bedford on 18th November 1976 and continued in this role for the RRE commitment within ongoing weapons development and approval right up until the aircraft's retirement in June 1993.

Canberra B Mk.6 WT333 arrived at Pershore in 1969 in its original B(I) Mk.8 build standard. The aircraft was temporarily held in storage at No.27 MU Shawbury between September 1970 and February 1972. It returned to

Pershore for reconditioning and modification to the long-nose design as well as modernisation of the navigation systems to make it available for anticipated AI or GW homing head research. On return from storage, WT333 awaited a low priority planned slot for a Second Line Servicing (PRC) with parallel conversion to B6 standard. The B(I)8 front fuselage was being replaced in this case by the three-crew bomber type front fuselage No.6649, initially built onto B Mk.2 WK135 and which, after three years interim use on B Mk.6 WT327, was finally upgraded with a full refurbishment. The airframe modifications included the incorporation of a long-nose monocoque and radome that was to be the fourth and last conversion to long-nose standard by the Pershore workshops. Unlike the previous conversions, the refurbishment and modification of WT333 commenced after the Government's October 1972 announcement that the Unit would close in 1976.

The news of that decision generated immense pressure for extra work by the bringing forward of other projects by the interested science departments and their major project contractors, knowing full well that there would be a significant break in capability during the transfer period with the inherent uncertainties to follow. So in this contracting climate, priorities had to be concentrated on all active projects with support considerations, such as the WT333 conversion, taking second place. However, by closure no work was to remain outstanding. WT333 was completed by the end of April 1977 and the aircraft was the last Canberra to leave Pershore.

On arrival at RAE Bedford on 18th May 1977 it was

immediately utilised for the flight evaluation and acceptance of the guidance head for the American Harpoon missile. WT333 was retired from active service in March 1994 at the closure of DRA Bedford.

Canberra B Mk.2 WK163 arrived at Pershore in April 1959 and its future role over the next three and a half decades was to be exclusively dedicated to radar research until final disposal.

In the early 1960s WK163 was utilised in the Pershore fleet to support two radar target projects. The first involved high altitude night flying for calibration measurements on the RAF early warning radar installations. For this role the aircraft was fitted with a high intensity forward looking light positioned behind the bomb aimer's window for ground observers to simultaneously compare with ground radar data, the light installation being supported with equipment mounted in a bomb bay container. The second project, in a similar night role, was the calibration of a satellite tracking station in Berkshire for which the aircraft's installation comprised a high intensity Xzeon lamp installed in a downward facing pallet suspended from the bomb rack attachments. The pallet's square lower panel accommodating the lamp formed the aircraft's external profile; cut outs in a set of dedicated bomb doors formed this aperture. The supporting equipment was in a self-contained pack which slid onto either of the rear cabin's two ejection seat rails. This easily transferable project package of seat rail mounted equipment, bomb bay pallet and associated cut-out bomb doors could, if required, be transferred to any Canberra.

Following a policy decision to introduce the new digital read-out navigation system, the rear cabin of WK163 had all the removable structures in the rear cabin stripped out during its 1965-66 second line servicing to facilitate design office access for implementing the redesign. The new outlay was fabricated in wood frames and hardboard panels as a mock-up for acceptance by all interested parties, after which the drawings were produced for the manufacture of hardware. In advance of this second line servicing WK163 had been identified as a long-term fleet aircraft. David Henderson elected to upgrade the aircraft to B Mk.6 standard by a straightforward change of wings, the latter accommodating the Avon Mk.109 engines incorporating anti-icing and giving 7,500 lbs thrust as well as 15% increase in power. The new wings also accommodated integral fuel tanks.

After this servicing, which introduced the first phase of the revised navigation refit, WK163 returned for flight trials as a basic B Mk.6 as carrier of two infra-red reconnaissance systems being developed by Hawker Siddeley Dynamics. The first system was intended for use in drones flying at slower speeds, the second system of similar technology but with added roll-stabilised multi-detectors was directed to the then future Jaguar aircraft.

In late 1971 WK163 was withdrawn to second line servicing for a partial reconditioning (PRC), the infrared development programme at that stage being transferred to the already prepared Viscount XT661, there being no break in the continuing scientific flight programme. At that time a high priority emerged for the unit to meet flight trials in support of the progressive development of the 'stand-off' reconnaissance system involving Canberra B Mk.6 WT327. To minimise the latter aircraft's preparation time, Henderson transferred WK163's already modified front fuselage (No.6663) to WT327, the centre fuselage of WK163 being removed for despatch to BAC Warton for change of the main (DTD 683) centre section forging whilst the remainder of the airframe was passed to second line servicing.

WK163 completed its PRC in 1972, having been rebuilt with its original centre fuselage, with new main spar, and the refurbished front fuselage (No.71399) formerly fitted to B Mk.6 XH568 but modified to the unit's final standard navigation fit. The aircraft then re-entered service as the back up to Viscount XT661 in the ongoing development of the infrared reconnaissance system. On 1st July 1976, WK163 became the first of the nine surviving radar Canberra aircraft to relocate to RAE Bedford in a phased transfer programme. After arrival it was retained as the backup aircraft for Viscount XT661. For over 30 years WK163 remained primarily a laboratory aircraft which supported the step by step development of infrared science as applied to the reconnaissance role. In the 1960s it was the proving vehicle for the Phantom equipment; in the 1970s it undertook the same role directed to the Jaguar requirement with the parallel involvement of the unit's larger Viscount XT661 laboratory aircraft. Finally, it aided the development of the Tornado Infrared Reconnaissance System (TIRRS) during the late 1980s and early 1990s. WK163 was finally retired by the RAE in May 1994.

The extraordinary use of the Canberra made by the RRE Aircraft Department was a direct result of the aircraft's good basic design features, which were not complex and afforded considerable flexibility in the positioning of experimental radar equipment. There were numerous options in respect of sources of electrical power and, above all, it was possibly the most reliable of all jet aircraft of its time with an excellent flight performance. The development of radar was not that of a specific project from start to finish, as in most cases of aerospace research. It was a continual advancement which rolled back the frontiers of scientific knowledge and in most cases was not necessarily focused on any specific aircraft type. Even at the project stage, for some military applications the scientists required only a representative 'platform in the sky' as an airborne laboratory which had the necessary speed and altitude capabilities, as well as on-board accommodation for a specialist observer. All such requirements were more than adequately met by this unique aircraft type.

*Plate 18 - Graham Hackett and Tony
Miller display XH568 to good advantage
at the RAF Cosford show in 1996.
Mark Burdett collection*

(Left) Plate 19 - WT333 and XH568 in open storage at Bruntingthorpe in 1998.
Author's collection

The CAP fleet

in its

various guises

(Right) Plate 20 - WK163 is protected from the elements at Bruntingthorpe in 1995.
Author's collection

(Below) Plate 21 - Doesn't she look smart! WK163 shows off her new paint scheme and new nose-cone as she waits on the ramp at Duxford prior to the Team's first public display; 8th June 1997.
Author's collection

Introducing the Canberra to Civil Aviation
Notes by Peter Gill, co-founder of Classic Aviation Projects

During 1993 rumours were circulating indicating that the Canberra was to be withdrawn from service and that 360 Sqn was to be disbanded. From our experience of aircraft preservation we believed it was worth considering saving one in flying condition due to its basically simple construction. The main problem was that the type had not been certified previously for civil operation other than by British Aerospace many years before. There was also the major difficulty that, due to its size, it could neither realistically be moved by road nor dismantled and reassembled after removal. Moving one by air was therefore the only real prospect and, as certification would be a long process, the plan was put on hold.

The real trigger came when the RAE at Bedford proposed to dispose of some Canberras at auction in July 1993. The real key was that they were offered with a delivery flight, which removed most of the delivery obstacles that stood in the way. It was always assumed that the aircraft from the RAE were low hours and well maintained and would represent the best option for a long future since the 360 Sqn aircraft were known to have had a hard life and were high in fatigue. There was also a magic about the famous and secretive 'Raspberry Ripple' aircraft.

The focus was then on XH568. We attended the auction but still with one outstanding major problem - where to put it? Undaunted, Frances and I went along to Philips in London still optimistic. As fate would have it, at Philips we met David Walton, whom we knew from our involvement with the Vulcan, and I boldly said, *"David, if we buy a Canberra today can we put it at Bruntingthorpe?"* He said, *"Yes."* and the scene for the auction was set. We were successful in our efforts but now faced a big challenge.

I will always remember our first visit to Bedford and meeting Richard Hall, the Engineering Manager. He had not seen us previously as we had not attended the viewing. He was a tall man and, swinging on his chair, he asked, *"What are you going to do with the Canberra?"* I replied, *"We are going to fly it."* The look on his face was worth all the effort insofar as he crashed back into the wall, which fortunately arrested his progress backwards.

From this point on the project gathered pace and the activities would fill a book, so we would just like to say that the help received from Richard Hall, Bill Johns, Terry Moore and Terry Griggs were major contributions to the setting up of the project and their commitment to it was outstanding. Many others, such as Chris Cawdron, Mark Burdett, Roy Burdett and Bruce Doughty, all helped and were later to become a major part of the civil project.

On the 19th November 1993 XH568 was delivered in grand style to Bruntingthorpe, where it was cold and clear with the TV in attendance. From this point the work really had to start. Preliminary discussions with the CAA had been encouraging and, fortunately, another project related to a TT18 was also in progress and the CAA ran them very much in parallel. The initial work entailed submissions regarding the accident history of the Canberra in service as the CAA needed to identify that, apart from military action, the loss rate for the type was no worse than would normally be expected. This work went well and was then followed by discussions on maintenance methods and practices, which systems in the aircraft would be maintained operational and how that would be done. There was considerable discussion regarding the escape and oxygen systems. In previous ex-military aircraft these had been inhibited and operational restrictions imposed. We felt this increased risk rather than reduced it so, after some months work, it was agreed we would keep them active.

There was also considerable work undertaken recording the actual history, maintenance state and fatigue life of XH568 itself. This took months and was not without some difficulty, but with dogged determination and together with the CAA, the critical document, the AAN (Airworthiness Authorisation Notice) was produced and agreed. This meant that, in principle, XH568 would be allowed to fly in the UK in daylight hours and reasonable weather.

The celebration was, however, muted at this point. The CAA had decided during 1993/94 that they were going to introduce a more formal regime for the operation and maintenance of ex-military aircraft than had existed previously. It was indicated that compliance with this provision, even then only a draft, would be a requirement for us to continue. This brought an enormous amount of additional work, the detail of which is not relevant here but anyone interested can look on the CAA website under BCAR A8-20 and CAP632 if they are considering a project such as ours in the future.

Enough of the negatives. With much help and many, many hours of work by a host of people, including ex-Bedford staff, in August 1994 XH568 departed the runway at Bruntingthorpe for its first flight as a civil aircraft. It was an emotional moment as the wheels tucked away and was the manifestation of what can be achieved by a small dedicated team of people sharing a common dream.

A considerable number of people had told us that what we were attempting was impossible; we can only thank them for that, since it only made us more determined to succeed. The success of the project, and the respect we received for this, enabled us to go on during the winter of 1994/95 to save WK163 and WT333 from Farnborough - but that is an even more interesting story ....

Displaying the Canberra - I
The Beginning - Displaying XH568 - A steep learning curve

After purchase at the MoD auction of 8th July 1993, modified Canberra B Mk.6 XH568 (G-BVIC) was ferried from DRA Bedford to Bruntingthorpe airfield in Leicestershire. In order to achieve Civil Aviation Authority (CAA) approval to be able to operate and maintain XH568, a limited company, Classic Aviation Projects Ltd. (CAP) was formed as a vehicle for all future activities involving the aircraft. For display purposes the aircraft would operate under the banner of *The Canberra Display Team* (CDT).

The initial visit to the group by the CAA was very positive and included representation from the local CAA office which would be responsible for ongoing maintenance aspects as well as the issue of the permit to fly. CAP was fortunate to acquire sufficient spares, documentation and ground equipment to support the aircraft at the time of its sale.

Discussion was held with the CAA as regard to aircrew licensing and this was successful with the nominated aircrew (pilots Graham Hackett and Dan Griffith) being eligible for the granting of exemptions for them to fly the Canberra in a civil environment.

Over the next twelve months considerable effort was expended by all within the group. A full airframe NDT inspection and systems check was carried out on XH568, a hurdle that the aircraft passed with flying colours and which had been no less expected! The Canberra was prepared for flight and after further discussion with the CAA the team was granted a permit to test.

The first civil flight was on the 7th August 1994. This involved a full air test flown by Graham Hackett and Tony Miller, together with Terry Moore on board. An

Plate 22 - Newly arrived from Bedford, XH568 poses outside the Butler hangar at Bruntingthorpe in 1994.

Chris Cawdron collection

(Left) Plate 23 - The team gather beside XH568 at Bruntingthorpe for the base's air day in 1995.

From left: Matt Farley-Wood, Chris Cawdron, Roger Joy, Frances Gill, Graham Hackett, Tony Miller, Nigel Scoines, Stewart Ross, Mark Burdett (kneeling), Peter Gill, Neil Lawes and Terry Moore.

Hilary Miller collection

intermediate stop was made at Cambridge Airport for fuel. The aircraft behaved perfectly throughout except for a couple of radio snags that necessitated a re-test, which was successfully carried out on 4th September. This cleared the outstanding issues and CAP was duly issued a full permit to fly for XH568. The organisation was also fully approved for the maintenance of the Canberra under the then chief engineer Terry Moore.

The first display season with the aircraft was in 1995 and proved very much to be a 'toe in the water' exercise with only a few displays undertaken. 1996 started badly for the team with the loss of their hangarage at Bruntingthorpe and having insufficient funds to cover the annual servicing. A plan was evolved to try and use RAF Wyton for servicing should the MoD be agreeable. Individuals within the group again agreed to loan further funds to cover any outstanding liabilities and decided that a considerable effort would be made to turn 1996 into a good year.

The plan to use Wyton as a base for servicing XH568 proved to be successful and the aircraft was flown in on the 22nd April. Servicing went as scheduled, so on the 17th of May the aircraft left Wyton bound for Bruntingthorpe. The first display booking the Canberra had for the 1996 season was the Londonderry air show on the 19th May. However, the appearance was cancelled by the organisers which had a knock-on effect with scheduled displays at Galway and Lostock. Displays at Southend were scheduled for the weekend of the 26-27th May, but the Saturday display was aborted due to bad weather. Sunday was better and the aircraft

made its display. The team displayed at RAF Cosford's show on 9th June, followed by the 'Last Great Canberra Party' at RAF Marham over the 21st-23rd June.

Canberras were to the fore during that weekend with XH568 displaying alongside an RAF PR9 and the private TT Mk.18 WJ680 (G-BURM) of the Canberra Flight. Marham was used as the base for that weekend with XH568 also displaying at the BAe Samlesbury families day. The end of June saw the aircraft display at RAF Waddington as well as the RAF Lyneham families' day. During July the Canberra travelled to the BAe Hawarden open day and at the end of the month the aircraft displayed at RAF Wyton and Bruntingthorpe.

On 1st August XH568 was down in the southwest of England at RAF St. Mawgan for the annual bank holiday show, followed by the Leicester air show on the 25th of that month. The final show of the 1996 season was as part of the Battle of Britain event on 12th September in the Channel Islands, with displays at St. Aubin's Bay, Jersey.

Generally, the Canberra Display Team's first full display season was well received by all who saw it (although the author does remember hearing the odd *"It's not a proper Canberra, not even the right colour."* remark from some so-called enthusiasts). Once XH568 was back at Bruntingthorpe, the team turned their attentions to WK163 with the intention of having it ready for the 1997 season. Although only one and a bit seasons were flown with XH568, the experience gained in display-aircraft operation proved valuable and would stand the group in good stead in the future.

Plate 24 - Sometime in 1995 the photographer had been lurking in the long grass at Bruntingthorpe awaiting the opportunity to catch XH568, now G-BVIC, just as the gear has travelled after take-off.

Brandon White collection

Displaying the Canberra - II
The Future - Displaying WK163

After servicing and a new colour scheme reflecting the aircraft's original finish of high speed silver (as well as the Napier Scorpion record details), WK163 was ready to face her public at the start of the 1997 air show season. Selling the Canberra started immediately with considerable coverage in the popular aviation press. CAP's operations manager Stewart Ross wrote to, and telephoned, air show organisers around the country. However, the air show industry was very slow on the uptake and interest was minimal, organisers preferring 'run of the mill' acts such as the Spitfire and Tornado.

This changed in June when David Henchie booked the aircraft for the Imperial War Museum's summer air show at Duxford. Dave has a soft spot for the aircraft being an ex Canberra navigator! The aircraft's display at Duxford was flown by Dave Piper and Tony Miller and was the highlight of the show for many that attended. The following day an air-to-air photo shoot was planned during the aircraft's transit from Duxford to Bruntingthorpe. Roger Joy remembered the experience:

"That was quite difficult actually. John Dibbs was using a Harvard as his camera platform and, as you can imagine, there's quite a difference in speed between that aircraft and the Canberra. Dan Griffith, who was flying the sortie, could only just fly slow enough whilst the Harvard was going flat out. I got a bit disorientated in the back because I couldn't see out, plus I was having to keep an eye on the speed and altitude all the time as well as monitor the fuel.

Dan, of course, was busy concentrating on positioning the aircraft with the camera aircraft. I had a fair idea of what John hoped to accomplish as we had briefed beforehand, but when you're actually in the aeroplane and suddenly you go into a manoeuvre, and you know you're doing something, but don't know what exactly, and then you see the speed dropping off, it makes for an interesting time."

The display at Duxford was followed by an appearance at RNAS Culdrose. The aircraft was flown to the Cornish base by Andy Rake and Stewart Ross but was grounded for two days due to dense fog and did not display as a result. The display at St. Mawgan was also lost due to the same weather conditions. It was, however, possible to carry out the record flight re-enactment in August from Luton Airport on the actual day, with the original aircraft, from the original airfield. *(See Plate 2)*

As an aside, whilst viewing WK163 at Farnborough prior to bidding for the aircraft in 1994, Roger Joy discovered that what he was looking at was the ex-Napier Scorpion Rocket test airframe, a genuine record breaker.

He announced to the team that if they were successful in their bidding, then he and they would see the aircraft ready to re-enact the flight on the 40th anniversary of the record in August 1997. A tall order indeed. However, as history proved, the group were successful with the event being commemorated in fine style at Luton Airport. Many people associated with the Canberra, as well as former Napier employees, attended the event. Old acquaintances were renewed and many stories were told about WK163 and the record attempts.

After the display at Luton, WK163 transited to Duxford for the following week's air show there. The Duxford show was the last outing for the aircraft in 1997, and with only four paying shows done, it was a big disappointment and a financial disaster. The team retired hurt to Bruntingthorpe for the winter. The lack of income forced the sale of the group's third Canberra B Mk.6 WT333 to raise much needed funds. Further funds were raised by contracting to recover the last two DRA Canberras, WT327 and XH567, from Boscombe Down that were destined for Air Platforms Inc. in the USA.

After the poor season in 1997, the start of the 1998 season looked promising with many bookings forthcoming. Word seemed to have reached air show organisers that the Canberra was a classic jet with a long and distinguished pedigree; and that it was an impressive performer as well.

And so to 1998 ....

The 1998 season got under way at Southend at the end of May followed by Kemble in the first week of June. There then followed three cancellations, which made the team wonder whether the 1997 season would repeat itself. However, this proved not to be the case; there was a steady stream of bookings which allowed the Canberra to display up and down the country almost every weekend throughout the summer as well as several trips to Belgium and Holland - including a fly-by at Schipol by invitation (almost a command!) from ATC.

Serviceability of the aircraft remained high but an accelerator control unit (ACU) failure on departure to RAF Waddington on the Thursday prior to the show prevented Andy Rake and Stewart Ross from attending the press day. Chris Cawdron, Bruce Doughty, Roger Joy and Stewart Ross worked well into the night at Bruntingthorpe using sodium lights out on the airfield. The problem was fixed, and the aircraft made its display time on Saturday morning.

The season also included an invitation to display at Farnborough 98. WK163 had appeared there in 1957 and 1958 whilst with Napier and it is the only aircraft to have displayed at Farnborough with a forty-year gap between appearances; a unique achievement. The experience of Farnborough was especially memorable for Stewart Ross, as he had first seen WK163 in 1958 when he had been taken to the event by his father.

Thus the first full season with the aircraft was a great success, although there were one or two interesting moments. Stewart Ross recalled one incident that happened mid-season:

"Andy Rake and myself took 163 down to the west country on 14th July 1998 to work up a display at Kemble, and then on to Culdrose to display the next day. As we took off into the display at Culdrose we got a nose-wheel red indication. The nose-wheel had castered out to port and remained there at 90 degrees off-centre as the gear retracted. No amount of positive g or shaking would get the wheel into its correct position so that it would retract properly. We did a low speed fly-by of the tower, who confirmed that the wheel was still locked to port but appeared undamaged. We went away and talked about it and decided that we had enough fuel to get to Yeovilton, which was our next port of call. It also had a much longer runway than Culdrose if it all went wrong!

We declared an emergency and proceeded to Yeovilton under control of St. Mawgan, our other diversion option. Hawk Red 8, of the Red Arrows, came up and did a close underside inspection and confirmed the wheels had moved to the 45 degree position and appeared to be undamaged and the tyres inflated. We thanked him for his assistance and bade him good day; with that he accelerated from underneath us, rolled inverted put the white smoke on and went on his way.

The plan was simple as most good ones are. On touchdown Andy would gently touch the wheels on the runway which should allow the wheel to spring back into place and all would be OK. The only worry was the amount of fuel we were using with the extra drag of the undercarriage, but it all worked out in the end. We landed safely with only minor damage to the undercarriage doors. That was failed display number two for Andy and me at Culdrose but we were determined to be third time lucky. With the 1999 show cancelled by international events, we finally managed to do a show for the Navy during the 2000 season."

Culdrose would seem to have been a bit if a jinx for the team over the last few years. At the end of the 1998 season the Canberra flew into RAF Wyton for its annual servicing in preparation for the new season. Towards the end of April 1999 the aircraft was ready. On the 27th of that month the team and the aircraft made a little bit of history when WK163 became the last Canberra to fly out of Wyton, a base that had been synonymous with the Canberra for so many years. The aircraft was crewed on that occasion by Phil Shaw and Stewart Ross.

.... and 1999

The new season duly arrived with many solid bookings for the aircraft. However the two big shows at Mildenhall and St. Mawgan were lost due to events in Kosovo. That being said there were some notable highlights in 1999. The Biggin Hill show was the first time that the Canberra had displayed there, and also the Fifties Festival of Flying at Coventry. Both of those shows were flown by Phil Shaw, who flew the bulk of the displays that season.

The best, however, was kept till last with the September show at the IWM Duxford. The theme of the show was a retrospective covering a century of airpower. The team's display was something very different starting with a new opening to the performance. A formation flypast consisting of Meteor and Canberra, Britains first jet fighter and jet bomber flying together again for the first time in over forty years. This was something of a coup for the team since the pilot of the Meteor was Dan Griffith who also flies the Canberra, which on this occasion was crewed by Dave Piper and Tony Miller.

The sight of these two aircraft flying together was not lost on the crowd and it was much appreciated by all who saw it. Little did they know that it had taken Stewart Ross and Dan Griffith two years to pull it off! The 1999 season had been a good one; as well as the displays mentioned above the aircraft also appeared at Old Warden, Southport, Clacton, Southend, Lowestoft, Kemble and Donnington. The 1999 season also introduced another new team member, navigator Geoff Burns.

A new home

The 2000 season would see the aircraft operating from Coventry Airport. With the return-to-flight project of Vulcan XH558 underway at Bruntingthorpe, it was apparent that there would be no hangar space available to service WK163. An approach was made to the Atlantic Group at Coventry Airport and, after much negotiation, hangarage and other facilities were made available through the generosity of the Atlantic Group chairman Mike Collett. After five years at Bruntingthorpe the team was on the move.

The weekend of the 25-26th March 2000 saw the team move to their new operating base. Dave Piper, along with Tony Miller and Mark Burdett, made the 5-minute transit flight from Bruntingthorpe with WK163 on the 26th. The hangar that was offered to the team was to be shared with the aircraft of the Air Atlantique historic flight; this opened

Plate 25 - The start of the display as the cartridge gets the crowd's attention at Duxford in 1998.

Memories of the 1998 season from the author's collection

Plate 26 - Perfect plan view! Andy Rake and Tony Miller show the Canberra's business end to the Fairford crowd at the 1998 Tattoo.

Plate 27 - Looking like a model aircraft, WK163 is dwarfed by Bruntingthorpe's massive runway.

Author's collection

From

Bruntingthorpe ....

(Right) Plate 28 - The British aircraft industry at its best - and both from the same stable. It would never get better! Bruntingthorpe 1999.

Author's collection

.... to

Coventry

Plate 29 - A foretaste of WK163's new home. Stewart Ross and Roger Joy refuel the aircraft at Coventry before displaying at Donington in October 1999.

Author's collection

up the possibilities of setting up shop on a permanent basis with space for offices, and areas for ground equipment and stores. The move would also give the team and Atlantic the chance to help each other in kind. A local haulier who was based at Bruntingthorpe made the logistics of moving all of the group's equipment easier, the entire move only taking two trips. The group has kept a presence at Bruntingthorpe, with Canberra B Mk.6 XH568 stored on site.

As an operating base Coventry is ideal; it has a 6,000ft runway along with a full ATC advisory service and fire cover. In fact, all the usual facilities associated with a working airport. One other facility the team has the use of is the Atlantic Group's operations centre, which has proved ideal for flight-planning the longer display transits that the Canberra sometimes has to undertake. The airport's main occupants are, of course, the classic freighters of Atlantic Airlines, with its fleet of Electra, DC6, DC3 aircraft and a whole host of other types operating on smaller contracts and company administrative work. The group's arrival at Coventry has added a new item of interest to the open days that are run throughout the year by the Atlantic Group. This is something the author can attest to, as he, as well as the rest of the team, was subjected to endless questions by enthusiasts that attended the airport open days that took place over the aircraft's servicing period.

Flight testing ....

The weekend of 20th/21st May saw WK163 flying from Coventry on a flight trim check after its winter servicing. The aircraft was flown for the 45-minute test flight by the team's chief pilot Dave Piper, with Tony Miller as navigator. Upon their return, the aircraft was declared fit with only a few minor electrical glitches. These were soon remedied after which Andy Rake took the aircraft aloft for a display practise, with Geoff Burns as display navigator. The final flight on the Saturday, before the weather closed in, was flown by Dave Piper, this time with Stewart Ross as navigator for his full display practice.

The weather was better on Sunday, so WK163 was airborne around 11am with Dan Griffith at the controls. His display routine never fails to impress, flying the aircraft as if it was a fighter. Casual observers and visitors to the Air Britain fly-in at Coventry that day had a real treat, an eight-minute routine culminating in a topside pass down the runway centre line, which looked almost as if the aircraft's wings were 90 degrees to the vertical. It was an experience for nav Geoff Burns too, who up until then had never displayed with Dan Griffith. He was enthusiastic about the experience:

"Well, that was an experience, I really enjoyed that, I'm going to like flying with Dan."

Dan was pleased too as he went through the de-brief.

"That was great stuff Geoff. That's just what I want to hear, height callout on the climb and speed on the descent; excellent, thank you."

The pair shook hands. After the jet had been re-fuelled and checked, Dave Piper and Geoff Burns launched for another display practise around mid-afternoon. The weather again began to close in, with the moisture in the air making wing-tip vortices during Dave's display as he banked the Canberra around during manoeuvres. These were quite noticeable with the high-speed run and break to end his display. The sound of airbrakes screaming in the airflow, followed by two white trails from the wing tips as the aircraft is turned hard, make for an impressive sight and sound.

.... for the Millennium season

The bank holiday weekend of 28th/29th May was the Canberra's first display booking of the new season. This was at Southend and was flown by Phil Shaw and Stewart Ross. The author met with them at Coventry in typical bank holiday weather; grey overcast, wind and rain! We dutifully got the aircraft ready and then retired to the airport restaurant. The weather seemed to be worsening, with the rain being swept across the airport ramp by the wind. The crew talked through their display sequence. The plan was to fly to Duxford and top up the fuel after doing some display practises there, then wait on the ground until they had a slot time for Southend. A call was made to Duxford to find out what the weather was doing there; much the same as Coventry as it turned out!

After a successful outing at Southend, the following weekend Phil and Stewart were due to display at Woodford on the Saturday. However, the trip was aborted because of the atrocious weather. Sunday, though, was better with the pair displaying the aircraft at Southampton for the Sea Wings 2000 airshow. A notable highlight at this event was the unique sight of WK163 flying in formation with a Hurricane. With very different flying qualities, the two types had to do a good deal of formation practice to make a safe display, particularly in the turns!

A week later on 10th June the team displayed at Ansty, Warwickshire, for the Rolls Royce families' day, with the aircraft crewed by Dave Piper and Roger Joy. With Ansty only four miles from Coventry it must hold the record for the shortest display transit. You could actually see the display with the naked eye from the airport.

The 17th and 18th of June saw Dave Piper, Geoff Burns and Roger Joy take the Canberra on an extended push to Ireland, with displays at Newtownards and Baldonnel on the Saturday, then Baldonnel and Enniskillen on the Sunday. They also managed to display at the RAF Cosford show on the Sunday after their return from Ireland; and with one or two organisational headaches whilst away it had been a busy weekend for all concerned.

Ireland was on the cards again the following weekend, with Dave Piper and Stewart Ross flying over to Bangor in Northern Ireland for a display over the sea-front before returning home. July arrived with the Canberra due to display at BAe Hawarden near Chester on the 1st but that was cancelled due to bad weather.

The aircraft was at RNAS Yeovilton for the 15/16th and was displayed by Phil Shaw and Stewart Ross. On the 19th, Andy Rake and Stewart Ross displayed at the mid-week show at RNAS Culdrose. At the end of July WK163 was at Farnborough for the SBAC show week, with the Canberra being on display in the Historic Aircraft Park.

The team displayed only twice in August; the first was at the Fifties Airshow at Coventry over 12/13th. This show was in only its second year and had already become a classic. The arrivals and practice day on the Saturday was superb, with endless blue sky and sunshine. The flying commenced on both days with the Canberra in formation with Meteors NF Mk.11 WM167 and F Mk.8 VZ467, flown by Dan Griffith and Rod Dean. It was a great way to open the afternoon's flying, the formation making two passes along the crowd line before turning away to come back in, head-on to the crowd, then break away to start their individual displays. The display content over the weekend made the Coventry show the best of the 2000 season despite the rain on the Sunday.

The Canberra was away again at the end of August with displays at Elvington. Then, in September, the aircraft was seen at the Shepway Festival crewed by Phil Shaw and Geoff Burns, followed a week later by the annual two day show at Southport with Dave Piper, Geoff Burns and Roger Joy doing the honours. Dave Piper and Roger Joy took the aircraft to Duxford on 15th October for the final display of the season.

An extended time out

At the end of the year there was a meeting of shareholders, and the decision was made to take a year off in 2001. The aircraft had flown continuously since 1997 and a large amount of work was required to enable it to continue flying in the future. To that end, work was undertaken on the Canberra until the start of the 2003 display season. During this time Peter Gill made it known that, for personal reasons, he no longer wished to be involved with the project.

It was at this stage Stewart Ross started to seek out other potential shareholders. Negotiations with Mike Collett of Air Atlantique eventually bore fruit, culminating in a deal whereby he personally brought Peter Gill's shares. On hearing of this development many outsiders assumed that the aircraft was now part of the Atlantic Historic Fight. Nothing could be further from the truth; the Canberra is still owned and operated by Classic Aviation Projects.

Flying the aircraft

Dan Griffith has been display flying the Canberra since CDT's first season back in 1995 with XH568. What follows is his description of what is involved in displaying quite a large aircraft.

"After line-up on the runway the rpm is set at 7,400 before releasing the brakes, engine acceleration is checked at 100 knots before rotating at 135 knots. The aircraft is then held level until the safety speed of 175 knots is reached. At the same time the undercarriage is raised and then the aircraft is accelerated to the civil climb speed of 250 knots.

When you are safely airborne the fuel handling must start and the booster pumps are switched on to get the process started. The Canberra is big, and it can be noisy and fast. Equally so, it can be quiet and slow, but it's never out of sight. The display itself is a combination of high speed and low speed manoeuvres, which show off the aircraft's best qualities; speed and agility. It has a very impressive turning circle which, combined with its large size and enormous power, makes for a tight, close, display. However, there are two golden rules when displaying the Canberra which relate to its large size and minimum single engine safety speed. Firstly, because of the large weight of the aircraft, its inertia has to be carefully managed, particularly when the nose is pointing earthwards so as to prevent a dangerous situation from developing.

Secondly, a sensible minimum display speed has to be set from the start due to the asymmetric characteristics of the aircraft. If the speed is too low the aircraft is unlikely to be controllable in the event of an engine failure. I use a minimum speed of 175 knots (full power safety speed) to keep me out of trouble. The navigator plays a key role in all of this, because he monitors the speed and heights, and will call out the next manoeuvre to be flown. He also monitors the fuel to ensure that all is well in terms of aircraft C of G. As the aircraft is so powerful, thrust levels have to be constantly varied to stop the aircraft 'running away' from you. The stick forces generated by the large changes of speed are predictably high, and swift trimming is required to make them manageable.

The normal display lasts around eight minutes, which seems like two when flying the routine. With so little time available, it is very important to use manoeuvres that flow well together in order to ensure that as many different attitudes and sounds can be demonstrated during the routine.

Once the display is over it is time to concentrate on the landing. Downwind, the speed is reduced to about 170 knots so as to allow the undercarriage to be lowered. During this stage the navigator will be

Al fresco flight planning

working out the correct landing speed for the remaining fuel. During finals, the flaps are lowered all at once and power reduced to achieve landing speed.

For safety reasons, it good practice to keep the rpm above 4,500 (to allow for single engine acceleration in the event of an engine failure) and the speed above 135 knots on finals. By doing so, it should still be possible to continue the landing under control, despite having an engine out. The big undercarriage makes landing a delight, with a touchdown speed of 100 knots. Although

the Canberra is fitted with Maxaret anti-skid brake units, braking is delayed until below 90 knots to reduce the risk of blowing a tyre.

Once on the ground and having taxied back to the parking area, it is time to put the seat pins back in and ensure the hatch switches are made safe, along with the undercarriage master. Shutdown procedure is straight-forward. The only unusual check is to open the bomb doors after the first engine shutdown to check the hydraulic system."

The navigator's lot

Geoff Burns is now in his seventh year as a display navigator with CDT; here he outlines what is involved from his position in the back seat.

"When displaying the Canberra, the role of the navigator is essentially unchanged from the days when the aircraft was in squadron service . Once a booking is confirmed, a route to and from the venue is planned together with any necessary criteria that are required for the display itself. The main difference that you need to be aware of is that the Canberra is governed by CAA rules since military rules no longer apply.

Route planning

In the civilian world, the navigator can no longer rely on there being a full fuel load on start-up. Financial stringencies dictate that a minimum fuel figure is in the tanks at start-up but equally, there needs to be a built-in margin of flexibility to cater for any changes to slot times or the route during the transit.

A 'straight line' approach needs to be applied when creating a skeleton route with the obvious doglegs and detours around controlled airspace, danger areas and Notams etc. From this skeleton route comes an initial set of fuel figures, and discussions then take place between the pilot, engineer(s) and navigator about the logistics of the day's operations. The pilot will have received details of the display hold points, timings, display line and any local area restrictions and hazards.

This set of base information is then used as a start point for my calculation of fuel figures and for agreeing the transit route with the pilot. A return transit may also need to be planned unless another transit is required for the next show. Discussions at this stage can be lengthy but a final plan will emerge and then you can get down to the task of chart preparation, route planning, fuel planning and the inclusion of any other contingency.

Flexibility and adaptability are key qualities that you must possess as a navigator. They are often invoked at short notice and it is not unknown for the plan to be amended in flight.

Pre-flight activities

Prior to take-off, the aircrew and ground crew need to arrive with enough time to carry out the requisite pre-flight activities. In general this means that while the engineers are busy preparing the aircraft for flight, the aircrew obtain the relevant information on weather and air traffic control. The Notams board is also checked for any pertinent information and then I apply all of this recently acquired knowledge to the route plan. A pre-flight briefing then takes place between the pilot and myself and the ensuing plan is finalized. On returning to

the aircraft, the aircrew are available to help with any outstanding tasks to prepare the aircraft for flight. This action is normally unnecessary however as the engineers almost always have things well under control.

Start-up, taxy and take-off

A 'challenge and response' system is used in the Canberra to effect the necessary actions during each stage of the sortie. The navigator is responsible for issuing the challenges at the appropriate time and for checking that the pilot has given the correct response. Additionally, I may need to relay details of the initial outward leg of the route to Air Traffic Control as well as noting any departure procedures that they require the aircraft to adhere to. Another task is to calculate two speeds for use in the take-off run - the Emergency Maximum Braking Speed (EMBS) and the STOP speed. As its name suggests, the EMBS is the speed below which the maximum amount of braking can be applied if an emergency occurs during the take-off run. The STOP speed is the speed below which the aircraft can be brought to a halt on the available runway length, although the brakes may then be burnt out.

During the take-off run I will make several calls; an initial check at 60 knots to verify that my Air Speed Indicator and that of the pilot's are reading within limits. The pilot is also monitoring the engine instruments, fire warning lights, position and status of the aircraft, condition of the runway, etc. and the take-off in general during the run. A further call is made by me at 100 knots and, as they are encountered, the EMBS, the STOP speed, the unstick speed, the safety speed and the undercarriage limiting speed if it is not retracted by the time that this speed has been attained. The aircraft is well known for its asymmetric handling problems and, with a 35 knot 'graveyard' zone between unstick speed and safety speed for the Canberra, there are only two courses of action available if an engine failure occurs at this stage. The pilot will be working extremely hard to keep the aircraft under control. If he is successful, the aircraft will be landed. If not, then we eject. Not surprisingly, the take-off run is a busy time with concentration levels running very high.

The transit

One of the limitations placed on the Canberra in the civil environment is that it can only fly within the limits of Visual Flight Rules. Consequently, the transit is flown at a height of 2,000 feet and at a speed of 240 knots. There are no electronic navigation aids in the aircraft so you have to relay topographical information to the pilot who, in turn, relays back any information about landmarks and geographical features. One option to simplify matters is for the navigator to un-strap and to come forward to do the map reading. The relatively

Plate 32 - Coventry in 2003, the aircraft's first outing in its new colours

Author's collection

short nature of any transits coupled with the need for the navigator to operate the IFF equipment generally precludes this however. Additionally, the use of a GPS as a backup medium can greatly assist with this task.

Fuel checks during the transit are critical and are another of my responsibilities. The flexibility and adaptability mentioned earlier come into play in no small manner during the transit and not just with regard to the fuel plan. On-going Air Traffic Control requirements may mean a change of route, the air show slot time may have been altered since take-off and the need to be aware of the position and height of other aircraft all help to keep your mind active.

Display routine

Having ensured that the aircraft has arrived on time at the designated show, you still have a job of work to do. The first task is to secure any loose articles in the rear crew area of the aircraft. Tied in with this is the need to ensure that visors are down in case of a bird strike and that all harnesses are tight and locked. It is essential that heights and speeds are monitored, particularly during a 'dirty' pass when the undercarriage is down.

A knowledge of the pilot's display routine is both useful and essential. Useful in that the necessary preparations can be made with regard to expectations of the aircraft's attitude and position. Essential in that speed, heights and rates of descent/ascent can be monitored. The rear crew area of the Canberra cockpit can be hot, dark and a very disorientating place - particularly during typical airshow manoeuvres. A strong stomach is sometimes needed to combat

airsickness and you must always keep the pilot informed of how much time is remaining of the display slot.

Landing

Once the display is complete, there are two options. One is for another transit to be undertaken, either to the next display or back to the home airfield. The other is to land at the display airfield in readiness for another slot or to refuel before the next transit. Either way, a landing will be required at some stage and the navigator still has a role to play. The prime role for the landing sequence is to calculate the threshold speed and to check that the pilot has correctly relayed back the minimum approach speed and the initial approach speed. The speeds are monitored by myself during the entire landing sequence. Only when the aircraft has landed, taxied in and shutdown can you begin to relax. This is only short lived however as the aircraft has to be prepared for its next flight. As before, assistance is given where needed and the cycle of activities commences once again.

In conclusion

The role of the navigator when displaying the Canberra on the air show circuit is demanding, rewarding and extremely enjoyable. The ability to work as a member of a highly dedicated team is paramount and a sense of humour goes a long way in achieving this. The Canberra is a remarkable aircraft and is supported by an equally remarkable team of dedicated and highly experienced engineers. As for me, to be a navigator as part of this team is a role which gives great pride, satisfaction and is a lot of fun!"

Engineering
'Generally the aircraft are very good in that respect'

During the early 1990s the British Government's policy 'Options for Change' came into force and would go on to have a lasting effect on the armed services of the UK. This policy also had an effect on defence research, with several establishments being closed or drastically reduced in size. With the closures and down-sizing came the inevitable retirement of some of the more obsolete equipment from within the defence agency.

In August 1994 a notice of intention of sale by the Ministry of Defence (MoD) was issued in respect of the disposal of 12 aircraft, a mixture of airworthy aircraft and training airframes from the Defence Research Agency (DRA) research and development air fleet. Four of the aircraft were Canberras, three B Mk.6s WT333, WK163, WH953 and T Mk.4 WJ865. Having already bought Canberra B Mk.6 XH568 the previous year, the team members looked at the possibility of a further purchase.

The aircraft at that time were still complete with trials fit, avionics and armament. However the tender was later withdrawn by the MoD as the aircraft had been advertised as 'sold as seen', and clearly they would not be made available in that condition on the day of sale. The aircraft were re-tendered in October 1994. The group decided at that stage to make an offer for WT333 and WK163; the plan was successful and in mid-November the group was notified to that effect.

The other two aircraft, T Mk.4 WJ865 and B Mk.6 WH953 were sold to Haningfield Metals who had helped CAP in the past. They agreed that any spares that were needed from the two aircraft could be taken for use in getting WK163 and WT333 airworthy again. In particular, WH953 donated its nose undercarriage shock absorber only a few days before departure when WK163's was found to be deflated. WJ865 donated its bomb doors to WK163 as its own doors had been modified to accommodate trials equipment.

The state of the aircraft after the sale left something to be desired. Prior to being collected by their new owners,

Plate 33 - Canberra WK163's port Avon 109 during inspection at Coventry in 2002. The area inboard of the engine houses the gearbox, hydraulic pump and associated piping.

Author's collection

Plate 34 - Farnborough rescue, 1995. Chris Cawdron monitors the engine instruments aboard WK163 whilst Bruce Doughty keeps an eye on proceedings from outside. The aircraft's nose-job is not yet complete!

Bruce Doughty collection

the Canberras had been set upon by the engineering staff at DRA. What the team found when they arrived to survey the two aircraft only complicated matters. Both WT333 and WK163 had been stripped of their trials kit, that having been done with little regard for the airframe. In addition, all the explosives for the aircraft escape systems had been removed. The way in which the DRA had presented the aircraft for removal from Farnborough meant much work had to be done so that they could both be flown out from their location.

Roger Joy remembered the first day of the work.

"We started work on WT333 first. When we first got to the aircraft the bomb doors were closed. We opened the bomb doors and all this wiring fell out and just hung from the bomb bay! We looked at it and thought this aeroplane isn't going anywhere. What had happened, of course, was they'd taken all the trials equipment out and just left everything hanging. So we had to painstakingly trace all the wiring to find out what was needed and what was redundant and remove it."

It was clear that nobody had thought about the possibility of these aircraft ever flying again. Work started in earnest during the latter half of November 1994 with the two aircraft being readied for their eventual flight to their new home at Bruntingthorpe. When the aircraft were sold they also came with comprehensive spares and ground

equipment which also had to be moved. The move from Farnborough spanned 14 weeks and the Canberras were finally flown out of there on 28th January 1995.

Roger Joy recalled the day the two jets left for Bruntingthorpe:

"That was quite a logistics nightmare, as we had to move both aircraft on the same day. The plan was to fly treble-three out first. We had a Piper Cherokee as a support aircraft, which flew the crew back to Farnborough so they could bring out 163. However the aircraft went U/S with a fault with its rudder trim mechanism. We eventually got in to Bruntingthorpe just as the sun was going down!"

Once at Bruntingthorpe those two aircraft were put into storage whilst the team concentrated their efforts on preparing their first Canberra, B Mk.6 XH568, for the coming display season.

Returning a record breaker to its former glory

A busy season in 1996 with XH568, meant progress was slow on WK163, but under the leadership of the team's chief engineer, Roger Joy, work on the aircraft began to increase throughout 1996. By December, the aircraft was ready for its ferry flight to RAF Wyton where hangarage had again been leased through the MoD to carry out the

Plate 35 - Close-up of the rear fuselage but minus its fin; Coventry 2002.
Author's collection

necessary servicing work. A ferry permit was issued by the CAA and the Canberra was flown into Wyton on 7th March 1997 by Sqn Ldr Dave Piper.

Once there, the work began in earnest. The aircraft was subjected to a full inspection and service, including non-destructive testing, (which is quite considerable on the aircraft) by Quest Inspection of Luton. No defects were found which was not unexpected as the airframe at the time of servicing had only logged 2,605 hours. Full functional tests were carried out with no problems arising other than a sticking air valve, which was soon rectified.

Whilst the servicing was continuing, various components were being acquired to enable the Canberra to be restored to bomber configuration. A new perspex nose had been acquired some time previously but it was without its internal fittings. These were found quite by chance on sister aircraft TT Mk.18 WK143 which was due to be burnt at RAE Llanbedr. Various other components had been overhauled, including the fire protection system which was carried out free of charge by Kidde-Graviner. Martin Baker Aircraft Company supplied two complete sets of ejection seat cartridges so that both aircraft could be serviced; once again, free of charge. The paint for the re-spray was supplied by German paint manufactures Ault and Wiborg, and considerable technical assistance came from John Griffin of Speis Hecker.

Once the bulk of the servicing had been completed, a start was made on returning the aircraft's nose to its original condition. The nose from its days as a Tornado recce system trials aircraft was removed and replaced with standard bomber nose glazing. Stewart Ross recalled:

"This turned out to be very time consuming as the nose cone is held in place by 148 nuts and bolts and

countless rivets. The end result, however, made the whole thing look as if progress was being made."

Painting was the final piece of the jigsaw and this involved the team in weeks of rubbing down to remove the high gloss paint from the aircraft's RAE days. During the paint stripping only three areas of corrosion were found and these were only light surface areas less than 3 inches in diameter. It took a total of 90 hours and many litres of paint, not to mention primer and other consumables, to cover the old RAE scheme. The paint was then left to harden before the stencils and markings were applied. Local sign writer Michael Murray of the Sign Workshop offered to paint the Scorpion motif on the aircraft's nose and then went on to produce all of the lettering too. On 4th May the Canberra was rolled out at Wyton for its post-restoration test flight, resplendent in its new colours.

The air test was successful, and after some flybys at Wyton, WK163 returned to Bruntingthorpe to await the start of the 1997 display season. On the whole, both XH568 and WK163 have been good maintenance-wise. There have been the odd glitches; for instance, there were hydraulic problems with XH568 not long after it was acquired whilst WK163 missed the Southport Sunday show in 1998 due to a fractured hydraulic pipe. Fortunately for this show, the aircraft was based at Warton for the weekend as BAe were also hosting families' day. The company afforded great assistance in providing the necessary materials and help to manufacture a new pipe, enabling the aircraft to return home later that day.

So far, that has been the only time the aircraft has missed a display due to a technical failure. The team's spares holdings are quite substantial and items are there when, and if, situations such as these arise.

Plate 36 - Stewart Ross and Geoff Burns re-fitting the fin section to WK163 at Coventry in June 2002.

Author's collection

Major service delays ....

Servicing prior to the 2002 display season was quite involved as all five-year life items were replaced on the aircraft; one such task involved the removal of all the aircraft's flying control surfaces for inspection. The fin was also removed as it needed a new fabric covering, this task being done by Atlantic Engineering.

Another job was to remove the bomb doors so that new seals could be fitted. A fuel pump in the bomb bay was also replaced at the same time as it was found to be unserviceable. Various redundant items from the aircraft's trials days were removed and some of the aircraft's original features were restored.

During this period the group gained a new team member when electrician Dave Bailey was recruited. Dave was then serving in the RAF with 4 Sqn at Cottesmore and came to the team with a wealth of knowledge and experience to do with Canberra electrics since he had previously served at Wyton on 100 and 360 Sqns. Since Dave has been with the team he has installed new power supplies for the aircraft GPS and fixed several long-running electrical problems. The author, too, was kept busy, cataloguing a new arrival of spares that had been donated by Chris Harris of QinetiQ Boscombe Down, the agency having spares recovered from PR Mk.7 WH779 prior to its being scrapped.

During this time, several companies within aviation supported the team; Kidde-Graviner once again supported the aircraft with the replacement of the fire protection system, as did Spies Hecker with paint and surface finishing materials. Del Hall of Survival Equipment Services at Kemble serviced the parachutes for the ejection seats and NDT Services from East Midlands Airport carried out the structural Non-Destructive Testing on the airframe. Dunlop refurbished the Maxaret anti-skid units for the aircraft's undercarriage back to zero-timed items. Atlantic Engineering and CFS Aero Products at Coventry also supported the CDT engineers who worked against the clock to get the aircraft ready for flight-testing.

.... and a fallow season

Even with all this work going on several areas of the servicing became protracted. One area included the issue of a mandatory permit directive from the CAA with regard to all civil operation of Avon engines. This resulted in Chris Cawdron having to carry out extensive extra work on the aircraft's engines. Chris rose admirably to this task and, in the process, produced a comprehensive procedure to satisfy the strict requirements of the CAA. As a result engine runs on the aircraft did not commence until early August. With the engine runs came the inevitable problems and subsequent rectification, all this extra work eating in to what was left of the season.

By the beginning of October the aircraft's ejection seats had been refitted after their servicing and the compass had been swung. However, display flying was not to be; the weekend of the 13th October arrived and with it the end of the 2002 season. So that weekend the team gathered at Bruntingthorpe and concentrated on removing both engines from XH568. This was done with the minimum of fuss with the help of a large mobile crane; the engines were then transported to Coventry for storage.

Thus ended a busy engineering year. Team members called it a day, safe with the knowledge that WK163 would be more ready than ever before to face the public at the start of the 2003 season.

Plate 37 - WK163 at RAF Wyton prior to its respray ....

Metamorphosis

at

RAF Wyton

Pictures by Mark Burdett

Plate 38 (above) and Plate 39 .... showing WK163 as the respray progressed.

A good season, but not without problems

The 2003 season was a good one for the team and there was plenty of 'Wow' factor with the aircraft displaying its new colours. However, during the latter stages of the season there were rumours of a new addition to the already-issued mandatory permit directive with regard to the operation of Rolls Royce Avon engines. At the end of the season the team's fears were realised.

Chris Cawdron* takes up the story:

"Due to the comparatively low utilisation of ex-military display aircraft, compared with their normal duty with the military, some concern had been expressed by various bodies in recent years about the relatively high calendar time which now passes between the normal overhaul periods of vintage Rolls Royce Avon jet engines. Traditionally they are limited by engine hours between overhauls and engine cycles for finite life, one cycle being a throttle movement from idle to maximum RPM and back to idle again. Following the investigation of an incident in 1998, it had been recommended that the calendar life of 20 years under military practice be reduced to 15 years regardless of engine hours or cycles. This recommendation became a draft legislation in 2000 with the issue to all private operators of Avon engines of a directive from the CAA to remove and overhaul any engines falling outside this new restriction before they could continue to be used in a civil ex-military aircraft.

Since the closure of the Avon overhaul cell at RAF Wyton, it has been impossible to get an Avon overhauled in this country and so, in effect, the legislation had prematurely ended the lives of some potentially serviceable engines and aircraft. This included both of the Avon units fitted to Canberra WK163.

Realising the potential loss to the airshow circuit of some unique aircraft, the CAA re-issued the directive in 2001 to include an alternative means by which the operators could comply with the recommendations. This would take the form of a maintenance programme encompassing thorough inspection of all the areas of concern for age-related deterioration due to long calendar time between overhauls. The maintenance period of 2002/2003 saw Classic Aviation Projects undertake such an inspection on both the Avon units fitted to WK163 and a full report was submitted just prior to the 2003 season.

It appeared that it did not fully meet the expectations of the CAA, although they had given out no guidance with the directive. The programme that CAP submitted was based mainly on 'in situ' internal inspection using introscopes to access the compressor, combustion and turbine sections of the engines. CAP felt that the inspection was valid and demonstrated that the engines

were safe for continued service. At the eleventh hour, and with the understanding that more dialogue was to ensue at the end of 2003 regarding the maintenance programme, the CAA granted CAP the permit to fly WK163 for the 2003 season. A successful season it was, also seeing the introduction of the popular Bomber Command colour scheme for the aeroplane.

In the latter part of 2003, with the aircraft now fully absorbed into the Air Atlantique Classic Flight at Coventry Airport, representatives from CAP and Air Atlantique met with the CAA Safety Regulations Group and other Avon operators to hammer out a maintenance programme which would be acceptable to all parties. The emphasis was on a programme which would encompass all Avon installations and not be aircraft-specific. It has to be borne in mind that the installation in a Canberra was far more accessible than, say, a Hunter, and so what would suit Canberra operators would not necessarily suit Hunter operators.

Eventually, and with the input from all affected operators, a maintenance programme was decided upon and work started to get the Avons through and ready to fly again. Our first, and probably the most time consuming issue, was how to support the maintenance programme with spare parts and documentation. We are the only operators in the UK of the Avon Mk.109 series, and we have had an uphill struggle in obtaining necessary spares and documentation to support the programme. This is the first time these engines have been dis-assembled to this level outside of the Original Equipment Manufacturer's overhaul facility. When WK163 and XH568 were in service at RAE Bedford, the Avons would be removed and sent back to Rolls Royce, East Kilbride, should any overhaul or major rectification be necessary. Therefore, the only spares or manuals which were transferred to Classic Aviation Projects on the purchase of the aircraft were purely to support minor and in-service repair or rectification.

Although formulated to avoid overhauling the engines, the maintenance programme encompassed overhaul 'territory' insofar as some of the spares and engine manuals we needed. Some of the inspection criteria we were required to follow was only documented in the Avon overhaul manuals and not in the RAF's In-service Manuals. We also needed essential spares to refit parts, which were not normally removed in service. We began a hunt for these parts and documents which was eventually to take us to some very far-flung parts of the world.

The saddest story is lack of support from this country. It seems that, for some companies, it is easier to turn their back on our British heritage and play the 'liability' card than to get stuck in with the rest of us. Our only motivation is to continue to preserve and display the sights and sounds of these wonderful and

Plate 40 - Shoe-horned into the hangar at Coventry for maintenance.

Author's collection

record-breaking aircraft. However, the support we received from smaller concerns in Great Britain and abroad is enough to put others to shame and has ensured the preservation of WK163.

It was necessary to remove the engines from the airframe to carry out the work. They were moved over to Air Atlantique's overhaul facility on Coventry Airport, CFS Aeroproducts, who kindly hosted Classic Aviation Project's work and provided much-needed and appreciated assistance. This caused a bit of initial interest as the Avons had no propellers hanging off the front of them; it must be remembered that Air Atlantique is synonymous with the DC3 and DC6!

The first engine, the highest-houred of the two, was duly pulled apart and inspected to decide what restoration and rectification was required. Not surprisingly, the internal parts were in a similar state to that which had been observed through the Introscopes before the 2003 season. This time, though, although the condition was reasonable for the age of the engine, we felt obliged to carry out restoration work to 'as new' condition as the engine was already stripped out and we felt it would better preserve the engines for continued service in years to come.

The workload was heavy and for some of the parts we decided it was better and more cost-effective to source and fit new than to repair and rectify in accordance with the overhaul manuals; which, incidentally, did not come from this country! During this time new procedures had to be written to document the work that had been carried out, not only to satisfy the CAA's stringent policies, but

also as the nature of the work was neither overhaul nor in-service repair. No procedure existed from Rolls Royce or the RAF which specifically covered the work we were doing and to which we could refer. It was, in fact, a totally new engineering procedure.

Almost two years from the final flight of 2003, after countless hours and effort put in by Classic Aviation Project engineers, and now looking pristine rather than a dirty old jet engine, the first Avon is completed and fully preserved for years to come. It is anticipated that the second Avon will see completion by the end of 2005. Most of the hard work finding the support for the programme has already been carried out, and WK163 should take to the air to impress the crowds once again in 2006.

It must also be borne in mind that operating this aircraft is not a seven day a week commercial venture. It is very much a voluntary weekend organisation still, but with much needed and appreciated support from the Air Atlantic Group at Coventry. All the team have been putting in long and arduous hours outside their normal non-aviation working days."

* Authors note: It is true to say that all the engineers who work on the aircraft have worked extremely hard in getting it to where it is today. However, Chris is, to say the least, modest about his achievements. He has worked single-handedly on the rebuild of the aircraft's engines with limited technical support and facilities. Having seen the standard of the restored Avons, his work on them is all the more remarkable. WK163 owes much to this man!

Surviving Airworthy Canberras

One would think that with the retirement of the Canberra, first from 100 Sqn in 1991 and then 360 Sqn in 1994, there would have been plenty of scope to operate more Canberras on the civil register. However, after 100 Sqn retired their aircraft they were not put up for disposal tender. Instead they were used as spares back-up for the Canberras of 360 Sqn. By October 1994, when 360 had disbanded, the aircraft that had at one time been with 100 Sqn left something to be desired. When the tender was finally issued in 1995 the surviving airframes, including those of the now disbanded 360 Sqn, were scrapped in quick succession. Two aircraft, both T Mk.17A, were spared the axe; WD955 (the RAF's oldest Canberra) was gifted to the Norwegian Air Force Museum at Bodo whilst WJ607 was sold at auction.

That being said, the 1990s saw the birth of several Canberra projects, some of which have been successful, others less so. Some operate on defence contracts or in environmental roles while others are preserved and flown with flying museums. What follows is an overview of the current state of civil Canberra operation.

Canberra B Mk.20 A84-229-N229CA
Palo Alto, California

This Canberra was the first of the type anywhere to be operated privately on the civil register. Built at Government Aircraft Factory (GAF) in April 1957 at Fisherman's Bend, A84-229 was one of seven Canberra B Mk.20s (licence-built B Mk.6) delivered that year to the Royal Australian Airforce (RAAF). During its 25 years of service the aircraft spent time with the Aircraft Research and Development Unit (ARDU), No.2 Squadron and No.3 Aircraft Depot 501 Wing. A84-229 did not serve in Vietnam with 2 Squadron, instead it served with the squadron at Butterworth, Malaya. Whilst flying with the squadron the aircraft achieved some 4,000 hours.

A84-229 remained with 2 Sqn until the unit was stood down at Amberley on the 9th March 1982. The aircraft was then held at Amberley awaiting a decision on its fate. Eventually, the Canberra was to go to private collector in the USA in a deal that would see a Lockheed Ventura go to the RAAF Museum. This was to be a very slow process, as the recipient of the Canberra, Aero Nostalgia Inc., although able to provide the Ventura was unable to collect A84-229. So the aircraft sat at Amberley between 1982 and 1990 at No.3 Aircraft Depot before a decision was made as to its future. Things seemed brighter when American collector Steve Picatti stepped in and purchased the aircraft from Aero Nostalgia Inc. With a new owner,

plans were made to get the aircraft airworthy for its flight to the USA.

The aircraft departed Australia on 11th August 1990, with all who had been involved sorry to see it go but with the satisfaction of knowing that the aircraft would be given the opportunity to fly once more, and that it would return in the near future for air shows in Australia. Upon arrival in the United States, she underwent an avionics and instrument upgrade.

Once the Canberra had completed its updates and had been approved for flight by the Federal Aviation Administration (FAA) under registration number N229CA, it was decide that it would make its display debut at the 1991 Oshkosh air show. It was at this show that the aircraft won the Silver Wrench Award, a handsome trophy awarded annually for excellence in craftsmanship and dedication in the preservation of aviation history. After Oshkosh the Canberra was seen at several major US air shows. During the off-season in the States, the aircraft returned to Australia in the summer months for displays and air shows.

Whilst in Australia the aircraft was flown to the capital, Canberra, for public relations work with the RAAF. After an eventful time in Australia, the aircraft returned to the United States in 1993 for the start of the US air show season. It was upon return to the States that the aircraft's fortunes changed with it remaining firmly on the ground, later to be under lock and key awaiting the outcome of legal action. It was during this time that the ownership of the Canberra changed hands.

In 1998 an attempt was made to fly A84-229 out from Boise but the FAA, due to various breaches in current regulations, prevented this. As the new owners were unable to fly the aircraft out they removed the wings, tail plane and moved the airframe out by road. In doing this without the correct equipment and knowledge the centre section attachment cleats were severely degraded. A sad end for an aircraft that could still be flying today if it had received the right care.

Canberra TT Mk.18 - WJ574 N77844
Van Nuys, California

Built as a B Mk.2 by Handley Page, Radlett, in 1953, WJ574 was ready for collection on 4th June of that year. Taken into RAF service, it was initially issued to 540 Sqn at RAF Benson. 540 Sqn's role was photographic reconnaissance for which it was equipped with PR Mk.3s but at that time only four of the type were available on the squadron as production of these aircraft was delayed by

(Left) Plate 41 - TT Mk.18 WJ680 as G-BURM at Cranfield in 1995.

Author's collection

Surviving

Canberras

I

(Above) Plate 42 - TT Mk.18 WK128 at rest at the Royal International Air Tattoo, Fairford, in 1998.

Author's photograph

(Left) Plate 43 - Ex-Royal Navy WK142 as N76764 at Fallon Field, Mesa, Arizona in September 2001.

Author's collection

English Electric. The squadron was loaned B Mk.2s to enable the crews to continue familiarisation and work-ups with the Canberra. After the PR3 deliveries re-started, the squadron retained several B2s until mid-1954 for crew training. Later the same year WJ574 was transferred to 57 Sqn at RAF Cottesmore. With the run-down of frontline Canberra squadrons in the late 1950s and early 1960s the aircraft was placed in long-term storage at 15MU Wroughton after its squadron service. WJ574 was sold to BAC in 1969 and allocated the manufacturers registration G-27-182. A further period of storage followed before the aircraft was converted to TT18 configuration and issued to the Royal Navy on 4th October 1979.

For the next ten years it flew as a target tug with the Fleet Requirements and Air Direction Unit (FRADU) at RNAS Yeovilton. Upon its retirement from service WJ574 was transferred to RAF St. Athan and put into storage. In 1995 it was one of several Canberras to be sold by MoD auction and was bought by Tom Foscue in the USA and given the registration of N77844. Today the aircraft flies on a regular basis and has recently been involved with Florida-based company Dynomat and their scientific research into thundercloud dissipation.

Canberra TT Mk.18 - WJ680 VH-ZSQ
'Charlie Tango' - Temora, NSW

Another airframe built by Handley Page, this Canberra *(Plate 41)* was delivered to the RAF in 1955 as a B Mk.2. The aircraft went first to 104 Sqn at Gutersloh as part of 551Wing. 104 Sqn disbanded in July 1956 and WJ680 was transferred to 59 Sqn, also at Gutersloh. Upon 59 Sqn's move to Geilenkirchen and subsequent re-equipment with Canberra B(I)8s, the aircraft was returned to the UK in early 1957 where it joined 35 Sqn at Upwood.

Like many other Canberras in Bomber Command as the type was replaced, it went into storage at 15MU Wroughton upon disbandment of 35 Sqn in 1961. In 1968 it was selected by BAC for conversion to TT18 standard. The aircraft joined 7 Sqn at RAF St. Mawgan in May 1970 when the squadron re-formed. Following service on 7 Sqn, the aircraft was one of six TT18s to be transferred to 100 Sqn at Wyton in 1981.

After eleven years with the 'Ton' WJ680 was put up for disposal, along with the majority of the squadron aircraft upon arrival of new equipment in the shape of the BAe Hawk. After a period of open storage at Wyton, Ron Mitchell purchased the aircraft and put it on the UK civil register as G-BURM with the idea of using it as a display aircraft. After the engineering work, which was carried out almost single-handed by chief engineer John Gannon, the aircraft was cleared for civil operation.

WJ680 was the first ex-military aircraft to receive its permit to fly under the new CAA A8-20 rules. Wg Cdr Rob Metcalfe and Sqn Ldr Dave Piper flew the aircraft at

UK air shows during the 1994-95 seasons with either John Gannon, Dave Moss, Peter Jennings or Ken Delve as display navigator. During this period the aircraft led a nomadic lifestyle being based at Duxford, North Weald and Kemble, where it arrived in 1996.

It stood out in the open until mid-1999 when a servicing team led by John Gannon was put together and began working on the aircraft. After months of servicing, followed by successful engine runs, CDT's chief pilot Dave Piper flew WJ680 out of Kemble on 7th January 2000 bound for RAF Marham. During 2000 the Canberra resided at Marham with work being carried out to bring the aircraft back into flying trim while a buyer for the aircraft was found.

After an eighteen-month stay at the Norfolk base, WJ680 departed Marham bound for Bournemouth, flown by Dan Griffith. Once there, a team completed the servicing prior to the aircraft being test flown by Dave Piper and Geoff Burns of CDT. On completion the CAA issued the relevant paperwork so that the aircraft could be flown to its new owners, the Temora Aviation Museum, in Australia. The aircraft left for Australia on the 10th May 2002 crewed by Phil Shaw (Pilot), Peter Dickens (Navigator) and Stewart Ross (Engineer) and arrived at Temora on 17th May.

To date, this is the longest flight under taken by a civil registered Canberra. The flight covered a total of 15,300 miles with a flight time of 29hrs 5min, the aircraft making stops at Genoa (Italy), Luqa (Malta), Heraklion (Crete), Hurghada (Egypt), Seeb (Oman), Bombay, Calcutta (India), Puket (Thailand), Kuala Lumpur (Malaysia), Bali (Indonesia), Darwin and Alice Springs before arrival at Temora, New South Wales.

The aircraft performed well in the varying temperatures that were encountered during the trip. An example being the aircraft's turn-round at Kuala Lumpur in heat of +40°C, followed 25 minutes later cruising at 45,000ft with the outside air temperature approximately -58°C. Fuel consumption was also impressive with the aircraft using 19,932 gallons of Jet A1. With the airframe safely delivered and registered on the Australian civil register as VH-ZSQ it remains to be seen how long it will be able to fly since it has such a high fatigue index.

Canberra TT Mk.18 - WK128
Canberra TT Mk.18 - WH734
Llanbedr, Wales - QinetiQ Canberras

Until April 2002 these two Canberras were the last of the type to be still flying with the UK defence agency. Based at Llanbedr airfield on the West Wales coast, the aircraft were used in support of air-to-air weapons development for the MoD. Built in June 1954, B Mk.2 WK128 *(Plate 42)* was, until its retirement in April 2002, the second oldest Canberra still flying; the honour of being the oldest (by a month) goes to 39 Sqn's T Mk.4 WH847. WK128 was allocated to the Royal Radar Establishment and served at Pershore on various trials from 1958 until 1975. The aircraft was stored at Pershore for two years until it was dismantled and sent by road to Flight Refuelling at their Tarrant Rushton facility in February 1977. Here it was overhauled and underwent a modification programme for operation of the Short SD1 Stiletto, a British version of the Beech AQM-37A supersonic target. In 1978, WK128 moved to Royal Aircraft Establishment at Llanbedr in North Wales were it has been used as a target launch platform. During its time with RAE the aircraft has been converted to TT18 configuration. Over the years the aircraft had been a regular attendee at the Royal International Air Tattoo at RAF Fairford.

QinetiQ's other Canberra, B Mk.2-TT Mk.18 WH734, was also retired in April 2002, it too having a long history as a trials aircraft. Firstly with Flight Refuelling Ltd. developing the Mk.16 Hose Drum Unit (HDU) for the Vickers Valiant; later it would take part in the first all-British jet air-to-air refuel with Meteor Mk.4 WE934 being the recipient aircraft. One feature on WH734 during this time was a refuelling probe fitted forward of the cockpit.

In 1976 the aircraft was converted to the target tug role, but despite this it has never been fully converted to TT18 status. The aircraft is very much a hybrid, being a B2 modified to launch supersonic targets, with other modifications to allow it to tow targets. This Canberra was flown on a rotational basis with WK128. Both aircraft have fairly low hours, 3,800hrs in WK128's case and WH734 with only 1,900hrs. Both aircraft were broken up for scrap in June 2005, from which the RAF recovered an extensive range of spares. However, the forward fuselages of both aircraft have been saved by collectors.

Canberra TT Mk.18 - WJ614 N76765
Canberra TT Mk.18 - WK142 N76764
Falcon Field, Mesa, Arizona

Canberra WJ614 was built as a B Mk.2 in 1954 by Handley Page at Radlett and was issued to 35 Sqn the same year. Over the next seventeen years the aircraft went on to serve with numbers 6, 85, 98 and 100 Sqns as well as the RAF Flying College at Manby. In 1970, BAC converted it to TT18 status and, on completion, the aircraft was transferred to the Royal Navy. Here, WJ614 operated as part of the Fleet Requirements and Direction Unit (FRADU) where the aircraft was tasked with towing a variety of targets for fleet gunnery training and air-to-air firing practice for the squadrons of the Fleet Air Arm. The aircraft was used in this role until the end of 1992 when it was flown to RAF St. Athan for storage, prior to being sold at the MoD auctions of 1995. WJ614 was sold to a buyer representing the European Warbird Organisation in the USA and was flown out to its new home the same year. The aircraft's history at this stage became sketchy, then in

1998 it appeared on the US civil register as N76765 registered to the Jet Aviation Historical Society in Phoenix, Arizona.

Another Canberra sold at the same 1995 auction was TT Mk.18 WK142 *(Plate 43)*. This aircraft was built as a B2 in 1954 by A V Roe, Woodford, and initially swerved with 115 Sqn. Later service included 207, 90, and 98 Sqns. BAC converted the airframe to TT18 standard in 1972 and the aircraft joined the FRADU at Yeovilton in March 1973. For the next sixteen years the aircraft plied its trade as a target tug for the Royal Navy. Upon retirement at the end of 1991 the Canberra was flown to RAF St. Athan for storage before being sold to a customer in the USA. This aircraft is also currently based at Falcon Field and is registered to the Jet Aviation Historical Society as N76764. Both Canberras have been stored at the Arizona location for some considerable time, now looking somewhat the worse for wear and it remains to be seen whether either aircraft will fly again.

Canberra B Mk.6 - WT327 N30UP
Canberra B Mk.6 - XH567 N40UP
Moffett Field, California - Air Platforms

Canberra B(I) Mk.8 WT327 arrived at Pershore from the Ferranti Flying Unit, Turnhouse, in January 1967. The new arrival satisfied RRE Aircraft Department's long-term requirement to operate a smaller Canberra fleet equipped with upgraded more powerful Avon Mk.109 engines. However, its interdictor cabin did not have provision for ejection seats for all occupants. Irrespective of Air Force policy on this issue, this feature was unacceptable to David Henderson who by 1968 had acquired a bomber-type front fuselage (No.6649), formerly fitted to Canberra B Mk.2 WK135. This was serviced, brought to the interim standard of navigation fit and used to replace the B(I)8 structure during WT327's second line servicing in 1969, thereby making it a straight B6. In the 1970-72 period the aircraft was initially the primary back-up for WK163 flying night calibrations with the Xzeon light for the satellite-tracking project. This was followed by a period carrying an experimental RRE-built lightweight Doppler system for basic research in this technology.

In the post war years, continuing research was focused on reconnaissance systems involving experimental work with radar, optical, laser and infrared devices. In applying this new technology it was found that the longer the aerial array, the higher the definition. However, aerials of up to 15ft in length were not practical for airborne installations and later research focused on future coherent radar with synthetic aperture aerials. This system was capable of detecting target motion by using signal processing to synthesise the effect of using larger aerials. This advance technology was called Synthetic Aperture Radar (SAR). Later on it was adapted for the ERS-1 space vehicle orbiting the earth to give pictures of astonishing clarity.

The various experimental SAR sideways-looking aerials under development needed to be lower than the fuselage profile line which, in turn, would necessitate the construction of a dielectric fairing some 18 inches (36 cms) below this line. It was recognised that such an external appendage might affect the airflow characteristics past the tailplane; this would need to be resolved. British Aerospace gave an unacceptable timescale for wind tunnel tests, which resulted in the unit's design office undertaking flow calculations from the Canberra's original wind tunnel tests to establish aerodynamic loads on the envisaged structure. Based on this study the intended shape was devised and an exact profiled flight test structure was made in hard foam. It was then encased within a substantial glass cloth resin-impregnated skin.

In the late 1960s this full size flight mock-up was suspended from the bomb rack attachments of WK163 for flight handling checks. The OC Flying was briefed to fly WK163 in a series of flights, commencing at 350 knots and increasing speed by increments of 50 knots up to the maximum of 450 knots whilst checking for effects of tailplane buffet and any effect on trim. The handling checks had been established within less than a month and proved that the design profile was correct and had no effect on the aircraft's handling characteristics. The manufacture of the new installation commenced to be phased in with the scheduled 1971 PRC of WT327.

The design of the aircraft modifications for the SAR reconnaissance radar, like all other project work, had to be transferable to any other variant in minimum time. In this case the installation, which externally appeared significant, was designed and manufactured as a set of an easily transferable package of components. The bomb bay was centrally divided into two separate areas by a profiled pallet whose forward bulkhead was enlarged to that of the aerial bay's profile, whilst its aft bulkhead was profiled to that of the standard fuselage. The pallet's own outer surface was appropriately faired between the two.

The pallet itself contained the necessary platforms to accommodate experimental equipment. The front bay of extended profile accommodated the SAR sideways viewing arrays and associated large dielectric panels and had a fixed forward structure of aerodynamic shape. The bomb bay aft of the pallet conformed exactly to the aperture dimensions of the PR Canberra flare bay to which the flare doors from the units Canberra PR Mk.7 WH776 were conveniently fitted.

The aft bay also had an equipment accommodation pallet suspended from the bomb beam attachments. These structural additions, which were fitted in 1972 without altering the aircraft's basic structure and were designed for removal in one working day for transfer to any other Canberra, lasted for over two decades on WT327 until the aircraft was sold into private ownership.

The electrical system was also upgraded during the PRC in which the port wing's auxiliary gearbox was modified to carry an interface constant speed unit driving a 12.5kVA alternator (acquired from the Harrier VTOL programme) to supply power for the SAR project's system. This box also accommodated a 6kW generator repeated on the starboard gearbox for essential aircraft services.

Research flying on the experimental SAR system commenced in 1972 and actively continued up to WT327's transfer to Bedford on 25th April 1977 where it continued for the Airborne Radar Group.

WT327 - a quirk of character

It is often said by many an aircraft engineer that each aeroplane has its own quirks and character. This is very true of old 'hand built' aircraft like the Canberra. As this was the largest fleet of one type operated at the RAE Bedford, it did not take too long to become aware of individuality amongst the ranks. Engine technician Chris Cawdron remembered:

"One particular aircraft has stuck in my mind, as I am sure it has in many a pilot's too. WT327 was to cause us many a headache and also led to a very unofficial addition to the engine starting procedures!

It has to be appreciated, firstly, that with all the experimental and research equipment which was bolted and strapped into every available void, the power demands on the aircraft's electrical systems were often quite large. All Bedford's Canberras, with the exception of perhaps the T4, were fitted with extra Type 515 generators attached to one of the accessory gearbox's spare drives.

WT327 was another exception to this rule as it was fitted with the huge Synthetic Aperture Radar installation that occupied the majority of the heavily modified bomb bay and most of the other empty spaces one can find in a standard Canberra. Needless to say, it required a special power supply to wake it up.

The extra amps were provided by a CSG (constant speed generator) which I believe was original equipment from a Harrier. This was attached inside the port inner stub wing and had a cooling system all of its own. The primary coolant was 'Sternol' and this was itself cooled by the fuel system via a system of pipes and cooler matrix blocks fitted in the port wheel well, which in turn required modification to the aircraft's fire suppression system. All this kit had pretty much been fitted by the time I became involved in the base maintenance hangar at Bedford. I was fresh out of my apprenticeship and up for a challenge - and, boy, did I get one!

Under the leadership of my two engine charge-hands of the time, John Stoddart and Barney Elsden, we started to scratch our heads over a particularly perplexing problem in that the port engine all but refused to start with this CSG fitted. It often made a very disturbing noise on light-up and this was mostly accompanied by a plume of white smoke from the jet pipe. If it did start at all, it struggled!

Anyone who has had the pleasure in firing up a Canberra will know that the initial starter RPM, obtained by the cartridge start, is crucial to a clean light-up and subsequent steady, controlled rise up to idle RPM. Any start under 1100 RPM, and you are most likely to see very high JPT (jet pipe temperature) and will often have to shut the engine down to avoid over-temping the turbine. With the port engine on WT327, anything under 1400 RPM and you could forget it. We were often changing starters after 50 shots to try to keep the rpm up; normal life is 800 shots, so that gives you some idea, and we would warm the starter cartridges before we fitted them to give them an extra kick. As an extra help, we ensured that the starboard engine was always started first (normal procedure is for port first) to pressurise the hydraulic system and take the load off the port hydraulic pump, which was also engine driven off the accessory gearbox. This also served to bring the starboard generator online to power up the electrical systems on other than just battery voltage.

In the meantime, we all pondered the problem, and I think that general opinion was that, as it was a constant speed generator, it was always going to be in an 'under speed' condition until the engine rpm had increased. So, in an effort to get up to its correct operating speed, it was imparting a huge drag on the engine at its most critical moment. Our main problem was the high JPT and so Barney decided to try to 'artificially' bleed off some of the fuel going to the burners to keep the JPT down and give the engine a chance to reach idle RPM without having to be shut down. This was achieved by trimming back the High Pressure fuel cock a little for start up, to divert some of the fuel to the overboard bleed. This did work quite well, but was a little inconsistent from what I recall and it did not do anything to reduce the drag on the engine and to increase the starting RPM. By this time we were still racing through the starter cartridge stocks and changing starters quite regularly.

The answer (or at least the best option) came from a suggestion from someone at Rolls Royce that we may try the opposite to what we were doing and to give the engine more fuel at start-up. This was to be achieved by partially opening the throttle (about a quarter) before

starting the engine and trimming it back to avoid over-temp. It worked! And it worked well. The only problem with it was that you would over-temp the turbine if you were not quick enough on pulling the throttle back. For this reason, Rolls Royce would not underwrite this procedure and so it could not be added as a 'local amendment' to WT327's procedures.

The start-up using this method was quite alarming at first as everything happened so quickly. The RPM would rocket up, as would the JPT, but you soon got used to it and worked out the optimum point to trim the throttle back to make the most of the extra boost, but also to keep the JPT down to an acceptable level.

The final problem was convincing the pilots to adopt this procedure bearing in mind that it was 'unofficial' and could not be added onto their reference cards. Some went with it; some did not which was understandable. I think this would all have been best avoided if the engineers at Pershore could have envisaged this problem at the design stage of the experimental fit and added some kind of pilot operated 'Clutch in/Clutch out' system to the CSG but I guess that is all too easy to say in hindsight.

The last time I had the pleasure (and I do mean that) of working with WT327 was a few years after the closure of Bedford when I got involved in recovering the aircraft from Boscombe Down to eventually go to its new owner Air Platforms Inc. I carried out the full ground runs on the aircraft and was able to resurrect our 'tweak' for one final time. I wonder how many cartridges would have been fired if I had not been there?"

These two, B Mk.6s WT327 and XH567, were the last two Canberras operated by the DTEO at Boscombe Down and were to find a new lease of life when they were brought at MoD auction in 1995. The Aerolease group initially bought both aircraft but they were later sold to the American company, Air Platforms Incorporated. Engineers from CDT were contracted to recover both aircraft from Boscombe Down, after which Dave Piper flew the aircraft to Kemble prior to their eventual journey to the USA. After some time at Kemble, WT327 (registered as G-BXMO) left for the States in December 1997, crewed by Sepp Pauli and Greg Aldred of DERA, Llanbedr. XH567 (registered G-BXOD) followed during April 1998.

Once in America the aircraft were registered as N30UP and N40UP respectively. Air Platforms Incorporated is based at the Ames Research Centre at Moffett Field in California. The company has been set up to service the airborne science community with safe, reliable, and highly flexible scientific and commercial aircraft sensor platforms

Plate 45 - WJ614 as N76765 at Falcon Field, Mesa, Arizona in September 2001.
Author's collection

Surviving

Canberras

II

Plate 46 - Covers on! Still in DRA service, XH567 under wraps on the ramp at Wideawake airfield.
Neil Lawes collection

and test beds. They can also facilitate the expanding requirement for medium- to high-altitude airborne science.

On 15th December 1999, one of the company's aircraft performed the first successful launch of a dropsonde data collection probe from an altitude of 50,000ft. This opened the way for obtaining operational data from the tops of tornado and hurricane clouds in that height bracket. The company has found a niche market, as the Canberras are ideally suited for high altitude weather penetration and overflight missions.

Both aircraft are fitted with GPS data collection systems and are capable of tracking up to eight dropsondes simultaneously. The specialist installations on board feature a nitrogen pressurised sonde ejection system, on-board telemetry receiving system and multifunction computer control with flat-panel display interface. The entire system can be controlled by an operator from the third seat. The aircraft's wing tips are adapted to attach either standard tip tanks or remote sensing instruments, and the wing hard points allow the fitment of additional fuel or large payload pods just as they had done during their time with the RRE/DRA.

Another project the company is investigating is the use of its aircraft for collecting data and infrared images on forest fires. There has been considerable interest from other countries in the Far East recently with regard to the company's operation of the Canberra in various roles. N40UP (XH567) recently undertook a proving flight to Japan in response to this interest. The company is also looking in to the possibility of modifying the wings of both aircraft similar to the PR Mk.9 so as to gain more altitude for weather operations. It would seem that with the advances in new technology regarding weather systems and earth environmental issues, there will be plenty of work for the two aircraft in the future.

Canberra B Mk.6 WT333 G-BVXC
Bruntingthorpe, Leicestershire

Though no longer airworthy, this aircraft is worthy of mention as its history ties in with the rest of this book.

Purchased by Classic Aviation Projects (CAP) at the same auction as WK163, this aircraft was destined to become a source of spares for the other two aircraft owned by the group. Like its stablemates, WT333 had been a research aircraft for all its working life. Built by English Electric at Preston as part of contract No. 6/Acft/6445/CB6(b) for thirty B(I)8 aircraft, WT333 was loaned on completion to Marshalls Ltd. Whilst there, the aircraft underwent work connected with an autopilot trials system. July 1956 saw WT333 transferred to the RAE Farnborough for flight development of LABS. The aircraft returned to Marshalls for LABS modifications prior to joining the strength of the A&AEE in March 1959.

A series of live firing trials followed with the Micro Cell rocket system. In 1965 the aircraft was on the fleet strength of BAC at Warton engaged in drop tank trials. Then in February 1966 WT333 was temporarily transferred to RAAF control for weapons trials at the Weapons Research Establishment (WRE) at Edinburgh Field, Australia. The aircraft was returned to RAF charge in July 1969 and was flown back to the UK by an RAAF crew who delivered it to the RRE at Pershore. A period of storage followed, seeing the aircraft at 27MU Shawbury between September 1970 and February 1972 before returning to Pershore.

Unit policy at the RRE prohibited any flight trial work in Canberra aircraft not fitted with ejection seats at all crew stations. So the Interdictor front fuselage was removed and replaced with forward fuselage No.6649 from WK135 that had been converted to long-nose configuration by the RRE (this work being carried out during the aircraft's 1975 refurbishment programme). Upon the closure of Pershore the aircraft was flown to its new base at the RAE Bedford in May 1977. It was from there that the Canberra continued its research work on behalf of the Airborne Radar Group Malvern. Towards the end of its working life the aircraft was involved in development of Laser Ranging Countermeasures System. This project saw WT333 detached to Quebec in Canada *(Plate 17)* and Holloman AFB, New Mexico during 1990.

Its flight test career over, the aircraft arrived at Farnborough for disposal tender in February 1994 with a total of 1,432 airframe hours. The aircraft was purchased by CAP Ltd. and registered as a B Mk.6 G-BVXC. The aircraft's final flight was on the 28th January 1995 when it was ferried from Farnborough to Bruntingthorpe. Within the year the aircraft began to give up its parts for the other two Canberras operated by CAP. In December 1995 the aircraft's port engine was removed for eventual installation in WK163, leaving WT333 engineless since its sale with WK163 included only three engines, one being recovered by the RAF. A jet pipe followed, as one on WK163 had been found to be cracked during inspection.

Then, in late 1998 the aircraft was sold to bolster CAP's fighting fund after the abysmal first display season with WK163. The new owners were two Worcestershire enthusiasts, Roger Wintle and Arthur Perks. Not having any plans to fly the aircraft, they decided to make it as live an exhibit as possible. To that end they have spent hundreds of hours restoring the aircraft to its former glory.

Today it looks almost brand new with its repainted colour scheme. Extensive work on the aircraft's electric and hydraulic systems has meant that the bomb doors, flying tail and cockpit instruments can be demonstrated, which adds a new dimension for visitors viewing the aircraft. Recently two Avon 109 engines have been fitted to allow the aircraft eventually to be ground-run. Whilst there are plenty of Canberra nose sections doing the rounds as exhibits, WT333 is the only structurally complete working exhibit on show in the UK.

Canberra B Mk.6 - WH953

Strictly speaking, Canberra B Mk.6 WH953 has no place in this section since it is not a surviving airframe but, as the one DRA Bedford trials Canberra not yet given any space in this book, it would be churlish to leave it out.

WH953 was, in the field of aviation research, possibly quite unique of all the 1,376 Canberra aircraft constructed. In addition to having continually served advanced developments in military airborne radar science for over 36 years, a considerable time span for any R&D aircraft, it was, in its later years, considered to be the most structurally robust of all Canberra aircraft since its fuselage structure had been extensively reinforced by the RRE Aircraft Department. This work had been carried out to retain the top speed of the original flight envelope when carrying future radar systems.

The aircraft, allotted to RRE in 1955, was the 14th of some 46 Canberra aircraft operated by the Establishment's Aircraft Department; its first project was to carry a new Air Interception (AI) radar intended for a single-seat fighter designated AI Mk.20. This installation necessitated fitting the scanner and radome on the front of the fuselage by blanking off the bomb aimer's compartment with a new cabin pressure bulkhead and fitting the radar head with radome within a conical profile.

The AI Mk.20 project, which involved both RRE and its sub-contractor, the E K Cole (EKCO) company, carried the code name Keen Willow. However the AI Mk.20 was dropped in favour of the later AI Mk.23 produced under contract by the Ferranti Company of Edinburgh. This latter system was intended for the single-seat Lightning aircraft which entered RAF service in 1960. The AI Mk.20 radar continued development in a revised form as the tail warning device for the V-Force bombers under the code name of Red Steer.

WH953 was then selected as the primary platform for the future development of the Continuous Wave (CW) radar technology, which would eventually replace the centimetric wavelength pulse radar so successfully. The aircraft was converted to long-nose configuration in support of this programme in late 1957. As in normal practice, the Canberra aircraft's cavernous bomb bay, with its fore and aft sling points, enabled the suspension of racking to accommodate any number of system equipment boxes and associated cable harnesses.

The initial CW radar, by nature of continuous transmission, necessitated separate transmitting and receiving aerials, hence the use of two wing tip tanks in the first flight experiments in Canberra B Mk.2 WF917 which proved unacceptable for eventual Service use. The initial phase of the project in WH953 was the research and development of a single dish aerial utilising an interrupter system phased between transmission and reception at a common source from which the CW function was

established. A number of areas of scientific development towards future technology were undertaken during this phase, which resulted in the aircraft being further modified in the early 1970s to carry the prototype radar for the Tornado aircraft.

The new role involved the fitting of a front fuselage radar head and equipment weighing up to 800lbs (over 360 Kg). Together with counter ballast in the rear fuselage, the centre fuselage section required upgrading by replacing the existing 'skin' with a pre-rolled 10swg sheet supplied by special order from the aircraft's manufacturer. In addition, the frame of the rear compartment escape hatch had to have similar reinforcements. This structural upgrade enabled WH953, when fully loaded at the extremities of the fuselage, to structurally meet the 450 knots flight case, and allowed flying at light weights through vertical gust conditions without the risk of structural failure. It also made WH953 the strongest Canberra ever to fly!

Trial platform stability factor; Canberra one : U2 nil

Towards the end of its working life at the RAE Bedford, WH953 was the main research platform for the Hi Camp (later renamed Music) trials for the American defence equivalent of the DRA, DARPA. Ian Kitson who worked on design and installation at RAE Bedford remembered the trials:

"The trials were carried out by DRA Bedford at the request of DARPA as their contractor, Lockheed, was having trouble getting acceptable results from their equipment that was installed in a U2. The workshops at Bedford designed the installation and had the equipment installed aboard WH953 within six months.

The first flight went perfectly, the equipment worked right for the first time since the project had started. It would later be discovered that the Canberra airframe was far more stable at extreme altitudes than the U2, and that was an aircraft that had been designed for high altitude flight! The Americans were so impressed they invited us to demonstrate the improved installation to their people. So, in 1989, we went on detachment with WH953 to the Naval Air Station at Alameda in California for two months which was most enjoyable."

DRA Bedford's involvement in flight trials was in three stages. The first encompassed trials in the UK which, as Ian records, were successful enough to undertake a second series of trials with DARPA, the deployment to California.

For the third and final stage the Music trials were continued in Australia in 1991, based at RAAF Townsville with occasional forays to RAAF Tindal for local trials in the Darwin area.

The journey each way required up to ten stages, visiting the Mediterranean, the Middle East, India, Malaysia, Indonesia and, of course, Australia. Epic indeed!

The Team

Sqn Ldr Dave Piper, RAF
Chief Pilot

Dave Piper flew Canberras with 100 and 360 Sqns and has been display flying the type since 1994. A current serving RAF officer and QFI, his service appointments have included OC Multi Engined Training Sqn at Cranwell flying the Jetstream T1. Until recently he was on the staff of the Central Gliding School at RAF Syerston. Dave is currently serving at RAF Marham as a pilot on 39 Sqn flying the Canberra PR9. With over 2,200hrs on the Canberra the 2006 display season will be his tenth year as chief pilot for CDT.

First Officer Andy Rake, British Airways
Pilot

Andy Rake is probably the least well known of the team's pool of pilots. Andy is now a British Airways 747-400 pilot having previously flown the E-3D Sentry at Waddington with 8 Sqn and the Canberra at Wyton with 100 Sqn. As a QFI he was an instructor at the Joint Elementary Flying Training Sqn (JEFTS) at Barkston Heath. He was the RAF Bulldog display pilot for 1991, and during the 1995-96 display seasons he flew the Hunting Bombardier Firefly.

Holding ATPL, CPL and PPL licences, he has been flying the Canberra in the display role since 1997. He has over 7,000hrs of which 1,200 plus are on the Canberra. The 2006 season will be his ninth year with CDT.

Captain Dan Griffith, Civil Aviation Authority
Pilot

Dan Griffith joined the Royal Air Force in 1982 going on to London University to study aeronautical engineering. His flying training began in 1984 on the Jet Provost at RAF Cranwell, later moving to RAF Valley to fly the Hawk and gain his wings. After the tactical weapons course on the Hawk, Dan was posted to 1 Sqn at RAF Wittering flying the Harrier. He was later posted to RAF Gutersloh in Germany again flying Harriers with 4 Sqn. After amassing over 1,000 hours on the Harrier, he was selected in 1992 for the USAF Test Pilots course at Edwards Air Force base. After graduation Dan returned to the UK and was posted as a military test pilot with the Defence Research Agency at Bedford which included flying the Canberra on various projects. He subsequently moved to DTEO Boscombe Down where his main project was flying the VAAC fly-by-wire Harrier, developing the next generation of Short Take off and Vertical Landing aircraft.

Dan left the RAF in 1996 to join the Civil Aviation Authority's flight department. He has over 5,000 flying hours logged on over 200 different aircraft types. Current display types include. Spitfire, Hurricane, Avenger, Sea Fury, Mustang, Vampire, Venom, Meteor, Hunter, Canberra, Jet Provost, Sea Vixen and T33 Silver Star. The 2006 season will be Dan's twelfth year of displaying the Canberra with CDT he currently has 160 plus hrs on type.

First Officer Phil Shaw, MVO FRAeS, GB Airways
Pilot

Phil Shaw joined the Royal Navy in 1969, gaining his wings in 1970. He has flown over thirty different types of fixed and rotary wing aircraft, and has over 10,000 flying hours. After training on the Wessex and the Sea King, he joined 819 Sqn at RNAS Prestwick for his first tour in 1971. He subsequently qualified as a flying instructor and joined 706 Advanced Flying Training Sqn. In 1974 he returned to front line flying with 814 Sqn aboard HMS *Hermes*. In 1976 Phil returned to 706 AFTS, where he was responsible for the organisation of Sea King flying training. He was appointed as a flying standards officer on all marks of Sea King, Wessex and Gazelle helicopters, during which his flying instructor's qualification was re-categorised to A1. In 1980 Phil was appointed as personal flying instructor to HRH the Duke of York and schooled him through his helicopter training.

After service as senior pilot of 814 Sqn aboard HMS *Illustrious* and *Hermes* between 1982-84, Phil returned to the examiners role until 1987. He completed the staff course at the Royal Naval College Greenwich prior to taking command of 826 Sqn in 1988. Phil was promoted to Commander in 1989, and in 1990 took command of the Fleet Air Arm tactical development cell. In 1992 he completed a fast-jet conversion course on the Hunter, followed by a Canberra conversion before taking command of 360 Sqn at RAF Wyton. Phil was the last OC 360 Sqn, disbanding the unit in October 1994. In 1995 Phil joined the Royal Navy Historic Flight, becoming its commanding officer in 1998. A posting to the staff of Flag Officer Naval Aviation followed where he was responsible for co-ordinating the introduction of the FAA's new helicopter, the Merlin, into service. Phil left the Royal Navy in 2001 and is currently flying as a First Officer on the Airbus A320 with GB Airways.

Current display types include Swordfish, Sea Fury, Firefly, Sea Hawk, Tiger Moth, Chipmunk, Bulldog, Piston Provost, Avenger, Jet Provost, Gnat, Hunter, and Canberra. With 700 plus hrs on type the 2006 season will be Phil's seventh year as Canberra display pilot with CDT.

Graham Hackett, RAF (Retd)
Former pilot

Graham had flown Canberras in Germany in the late 1960s before going on to fly RAF Buccaneers. His experience on both types stood him in good stead at RAE Bedford, since the AI radar for the Tornado fleet was being trialled in Radar Research Squadron's Buccaneer.

Graham left DRA just before Bedford's closure to fly from Cambridge for Suckling Airways as well as being the team's only pilot in the early days. Ultimately Graham took a job flying HS125s in Nigeria, so bowed out of his involvement with display flying.

Tony 'Dusty' Miller, RAF (Retd)
Navigator

Until 2002 Tony was probably the navigator with the longest flying connection with the Canberra, having joined the RAF in 1964 and flown the aircraft in one guise or another from 1966 until moving away to Somerset in 2002. His first Canberra squadron was No.31, flying PR7s at RAF Laarbruch, followed by 360 Sqn and 231 OCU at RAF Cottesmore. The OCU stint was very short - some six months - before he and Norman Gill were initially seconded, and subsequently posted, as a crew to 13 Sqn, RAF Luqa, to establish a conversion course for crews arriving as the squadron re-equipped with PR7s. The squadron was reluctant to relinquish its PR9s, however, so it operated a mixed fleet of PR7s and PR9s for the remainder of Tony's stay in Malta. There was many a happy, but busy, hour strapped into the nose of a PR9!

In May 1975 he resumed life as an OCU instructor on 231 OCU at RAF Cottesmore, then Marham, before moving to RAF Wyton as Wing Photo Leader in late 1977, albeit still with occasional flying duties. Next job, in 1981, was with 39 Sqn and No.1 PRU at Wyton before returning to 231 OCU in 1984. A year was spent with 51 Sqn before moving to Radar Research Sqn at RAE Bedford in 1987.

Tony ended his RAF career at Bedford when flying ceased there in 1994, during which time he had crewed all of Bedford's fleet including Buccaneer, Tornado and, just once, the Harrier! There followed some five years of aerial photography around the UK, interspersed with display flying with CDT, which he hopes to resume in 2006.

Geoff Burns, RAF (Retd)
Navigator

Geoff Burns joined the RAF in 1970 and after completing training as a navigator gained his brevet in 1972. After converting on to the Canberra he was posted to 7 Sqn at RAF St. Mawgan. Geoff's introduction to Canberra flying was somewhat unusual in that ten days after arrival on the Squadron he had to eject from Canberra TT Mk.18 WJ680, when the aircraft's rudder became partly detached from its fin during a post-minor air test!

Apart from the routine Target Facilities taskings on the squadron, there were highlights during his first tour. One of which was being part of the crew that located missing round the world yachtsman Cdr King in 1973. Geoff left 7 Sqn in October 1975. A brief interlude from flying followed as families' officer at RAF Buchan. In March 1976 he was back on Canberras with a posting to 231 OCU at RAF Marham as a supernumerary staff navigator. Life on the OCU was more formal than being on a Sqn, however the occasional sortie as a navigator with 100 Sqn interspersed with flying with foreign crews coming through the syllabus helped to break up the routine of the OCU. Supernumerary status also allowed him to continue taking part in joint forces exercises. He left the OCU and the air force in September 1977. His involvement with the Canberra ended there, and it was not until 1998 that a chance meeting with Dave Piper and Tony Miller at Duxford led to an invitation to join CDT as a second display navigator. Geoff made his display debut at the Southend airshow at the start of the 1999 season.

Aircraft types include Varsity, Dominie T1, Jet Provost, Chipmunk and Tiger Moth. Canberra marks include T4, B2, TT18 and T19. With 1,300 hrs on type the 2006 display season will be Geoff's seventh year as Canberra display navigator with CDT.

Stewart Ross
Operations Manager and engineer

Stewart Ross joined the RAF in April 1966 as a photographer. After trade training at RAF Cosford he was posted in May 1967 to the Bomber Command NDT Unit at RAF Cottesmore. September 1968 saw Stewart posted to RAF Luqa firstly with 13 Sqn working with the Canberra PR9, then later moving 'down the pan' to 39 Sqn, again with the PR9. After two and a half years in Malta he was posted in March 1971 to JARIC at RAF Brampton. October 1971 saw Stewart back at RAF Cosford for an Air Camera Fitters course. In June 1972 he was posted to RAF Wyton and back to the Canberras of 39 Sqn. Whilst at Wyton he was detached in November 1972 to the A&AEE at Boscombe Down for photographic equipment trials.

Stewart was posted to RAF Wildenrath in November 1973 firstly with 20 Sqn working with the Harrier GR1A, then in January 1974 he moved across to 60 Sqn working on, and flying in, the Pembroke C(PR)1. November 1976 saw him on the move again this time to RAF Kinloss and 206 Sqn flying as crew on the Nimrod MR2. Stewart was not at Kinloss long as in November 1977 he was posted back to 39 Sqn at Wyton again on the Canberra PR9. He stayed with 39 Sqn until leaving the RAF in July 1979. The 2006 display season is Stewart's twelfth year as display operations manager for CDT.

Roger Joy
Airframes and former Chief Engineer

Roger Joy joined the Royal Air Force in September 1963. After three years as an apprentice at RAF Halton, he was posted in 1966 to 214 Sqn on the HP Victor K1 at RAF Marham. Eighteen months later he was on the move again with his first overseas tour with 39 Sqn at RAF Luqa, Malta, working on the Canberra PR9. In 1970 39 Sqn moved back to the UK and were based at RAF Wyton where Roger worked on squadron first and second line servicing. In 1974 he was posted to RAF Lossiemouth and 226 OCU working on the then new BAC/Sepecat Jaguar.

After four years with the OCU Roger was again posted back to RAF Wyton and the station AEF (Aircraft Engineering Flight). The flight's remit also included operating DH Devon's on VIP duties as well as acting as the Wyton station flight operating such diverse types as the HS Andover and Jet Provost Mk.5. The flight also had responsibility for the station's two Canberra T4s.

In 1980 Roger was overseas again, this time a three year tour with the Kuwait liaison team covering NDT with the Kuwait Air Force. During his time with the KAF he worked on such types as the A4 Skyhawk, Mirage F1, BAC Strikemaster, C130 Hercules and McDonnell Douglas DC9. On his return from Kuwait in 1983 Roger was posted to RAF Waddington and the ill-fated Nimrod AEW3 programme. After the collapse of the AEW3 programme he found himself at RAF Linton-on-Ouse helping with the civilian contract handover of the station. An exchange posting in 1984 saw Roger back at RAF Wyton and on the Canberras of 100 Sqn. He stayed with 100 Sqn until he left the RAF in 1989.

A principal member of the team since its inception, Roger has recently stepped down as Chief Engineer to allow himself more time to devote to other projects.

Chris Cawdron
Propulsion and Deputy Engineering Manager

Chris started a four year apprenticeship at RAE Bedford (Thurleigh) in September 1985 and trained as an Airframe-Engine Craftsman. He spent two years in the Apprentice School following a new 'Standards Based Syllabus' and then went over to the Establishment hangars to work along side Apprentice Masters and carry out the daily tasks in a hanger environment. During this period, Chris realised that his interest in jet engines would go on to shape his career and he made it known that this was to be his chosen trade.

In the following two years, Chris spent time in most of the related workshops covering hydraulic, wheel, electrical and NDT to gain an appreciation of the other trades involved. His apprenticeship finished in 1989 and he was given the position of Engine Craftsman involved in second and third line servicing and became an Apprentice Master himself. His training in airframes was also utilised to a lesser extent. Extending his college studies for an extra year, Chris achieved a BTEC HNC in Aerospace Engineering with distinctions in 'Propulsion Technology' and 'Aircraft Controls and Instrumentation'.

During his remaining years at the RAE, Chris worked on a multitude of aircraft types including Canberra, Harrier, Buccaneer, Hawk, Tornado, HS748, Andover, Viscount, BAC1-11 and also helicopters such as the Lynx, Wessex, Sea King and Gazelle. Chris also clocked up many hours ground testing, especially on the Canberra fleet, and went on to learn the idiosyncrasies of Rolls Royce Avon 109 engines. He later spent two years in the Establishment's Flight Hangar involved in first line servicing, again with the Canberra being the most prevalent type.

Chris was first involved with Classic Aviation after meeting Peter and Francis Gill a few days after they had purchased Canberra B Mk.6 XH568 (G-BVIC). He offered his support and assistance in re-homing the aircraft and also carried out some pending modifications in his spare time prior to the delivery flight. Chris stayed at Bedford for nine years until its closure in 1994; he now works at Cosworth Technology at Northampton where he is a 'Principal Engine Build Technician'. Deputising to the Engine Build Shop Supervisor, his main duties involve producing prototype engine assembly manuals, co-ordinating inspection and assembly of prototype and durability engines as well as designing and drafting prototype engine assembly tooling. A founder member of the engineering team, the 2006 season will be his twelfth year with CDT.

Mark Burdett
Armourer

Mark Burdett joined the Royal Air Force in September 1980. After completing trade training at RAF Cosford as an armourer he was posted to 16 MU Stafford working between the Gun Bay and Station Armoury. In 1983 he was posted to 233 Harrier OCU at Wittering where he worked on weapon systems associated with the Harrier GR3. After leaving the RAF, Mark joined RAE Bedford in 1987. It was a fulfilment of a boyhood dream for him. Growing up near Bedford airfield he used to cycle there in the school holidays to watch the aircraft test fleet, never thinking he would end up working there some 15 years later. Mark recalls that outdoor games lessons at school were always a good chance to spot strangely coloured Sea Vixens and Canberras! Whilst as Bedford he worked on the ejection systems for the unit's Tornado, Buccaneer, Hawk and Canberra aircraft.

Involved with the Canberra Display Team from the beginning, Mark is unique in being the only qualified armorer within any private group operating ex-military jets. For him, he sees his work on the Canberra as a tribute to all ex-Bedford colleagues especially the late Gordon Tuffnail and Ivan O'Prey, Armament Supervisors. Finally, he says that the aircraft is probably one of the nicest machines he has worked on over the years, next to his 1974 Reliant Scimitar! He is now in his twelfth year as armourer for CDT.

Bruce Doughty
Airframes and Engineering Manager

Bruce Doughty started a four year apprenticeship at the Royal Aircraft Establishment Bedford (Thurleigh) in September 1977. The apprenticeship included the joint trades of airframe and engines. Other areas covered in the apprenticeship were hydraulic servicing, Non-Destructive Testing, basic electric and fabric work. During the third and fourth years of the apprenticeship he worked in the various hangers under Apprentice Masters. The majority of his time was spent in the Establishment's Hangar No.1 where minor, major and experimental installations were carried out. After the apprenticeship he took a position as an airframe fitter, concentrating on second and third line servicing on all types of aircraft including the Canberra.

Later he worked on civil aircraft types and became an Apprentice Master. In 1988 he was promoted to PTO grade in the Non-Destructive Testing Department. He took courses at the RAF school of Non-Destructive Testing at RAF Swanton Morley in Norfolk in 1989, followed by six months hands-on training at Bedford to fully qualify as Q-A-NDT. In the NDT section he was also responsible for EFDC, a calibration cell for torque wrenches, pressure gauges and metal hardness testing, Bruce also undertook training for helicopter rotor blade tracking, balancing and vibration analysis.

During this time there was a variety of NDT work, covering not only the Bedford fleet, but also RAE Llanbedr's Canberras and the Martin Baker Meteor; also there were occasional jobs to be done for the Shuttleworth Collection. Over the years he has worked on a wide variety of military and civil aircraft and helicopters. In his last year at RAE Bedford he was supervisor of the Establishment's No.1 Hangar, and it was during this period that that he met Peter and Francis Gill when he handed over the relevant NDT records for WK163.

He did not know that he would work on Canberras again until he met with ex-Bedford colleague Chris Cawdron, who introduced him to the team and he was invited to join. Bruce left RAE Bedford upon its closure in 1994 after sixteen years service. He worked for Cosworth Racing in Northampton involved with production engineering of engine parts for Indy-car, Jaguar Formula One engines and Aprilia racing bikes. Since January 2005 Bruce has been a full time engineer with Air Atlantique and the 2006 display season will be his twelfth with CDT.

Dave Bailey
Electrician

Dave is currently employed as an Air Electrical Engineering Technician in the Royal Air Force. He has been in the RAF for 18 years and holds the rank of Sergeant. He is presently employed on IV (AC) Sqn stationed at RAF Cottesmore, where he carries out scheduled maintenance and rectification on the squadron's Harrier GR7 and T10 aircraft. During his time in the Air Force he has also worked on the Jaguar with 54 Sqn, the Puma with 1563 Flt in Belize as well as various other aircraft as a member of a Station Visiting Aircraft Section.

Dave has worked on Canberras during two of his tours. His first was with 100 Sqn, between 1984-1988, employed on Canberra B2, E15, PR7 and TT18 aircraft. His second tour was from 1992 -1993 with 360 Sqn employed on T17, T17A, PR7, T4 and B2 (T) aircraft. Here he was employed on first and second line maintenance as an electrical technician carrying out and supervising maintenance, fault diagnosis and rectification on Canberra electrical systems. Dave joined the engineering team at the end of 2001; the 2006 season will be his fifth year with the Canberra Display Team.

Dave Jackson
Engineering Support and Team Archivist

Dave joined the Royal Air Force in 1990 but, unlike the rest of the team, does not have an aircraft trade background, electing instead to serve as RAF Policeman. After trade training he was posted in April 1991 to RAF Honington were he was involved in security operations in support of the Tornado Weapons Conversion Unit and No.13 Sqn. July 1992 saw him posted to RAF Bruggen in Germany, again on security operations supporting the Tornado squadrons of the Bruggen wing.

In July 1995 he was posted to Headquarters Strike Command at RAF High Wycombe and attached to the security staff of NATO C in C Allied Forces North West Europe. He left the RAF in September 1999.

Although not from an aircraft engineering background, Dave grew up in the shadow of aviation as an Air Force 'Scalie Brat' and has held an interest in the subject from an early age. He was a member of the Duxford Aviation Society between 1991-99 and worked as a volunteer on many of the exhibits that are held by the Imperial War Museum at Duxford. During his time with the DAS he acquired many new skills in relation to working on aircraft. Since 1998 he has been photographing and writing about aviation-related subjects for publication. He was invited to join the team at the end of the 1999 season to look after engineering support; he is also the group archivist. The 2006 display season will be his seventh year with the Canberra Display Team.

Appendix 1
Abbreviations

ASM	Armstrong Siddeley Motors Ltd		MRF	Meteorological Research Flight
ARG	Airborne Radar Group		MoS	Ministry of Supply
A&AEE	Aircraft and Armament Evaluation Establishment		MPD	Mandatory Permit Directive
			MRCA	Multi Role Combat Aircraft
ATDU	Air Torpedo Development Unit		MU	Maintenance Unit
AFB	Air Force Base		NAS	Naval Air Station
AA	Air Atlantique		NDT	Non Destructive Testing
ADF	Automatic Direction Finding		NF	Night Fighter
AI	Air Interception		PRC	Partial Reconditioning / Paste Sealant
ASV	Air to Surface Vessel		PWI	Preliminary Warning Instruction
BAC	British Aircraft Corporation		RRE	Royal Radar Establishment
BAe	British Aerospace / BAe Systems		RAE	Royal Aircraft Establishment
BLEU	Blind Landing Experimental Unit		RDF	Radio Direction Finding
CAA	Civil Aviation Authority		RRFU	Radar Research Flying Unit
CAP	Classic Aviation Projects		SI	Servicing Instruction
CDT	Canberra Display Team		STI	Special Technical Instruction
CT	Continuation Training		SAR	Synthetic Aperture Radar
DRA	Defence Research Agency		SSR	Secondary Surveillance Radar
DERA	Defence Evaluation Research Agency		SCR	Signals Corps Radar
DTEO	Defence Test Evaluation Organisation		SDF	Special Duties Flight
DARPA	Defence Advanced Research Projects Agency		TRE	Telecommunications Research Establishment
DANAC	Decca Area Navigation Airborne Computer		TANS	Tactical Air Navigation System
DTD	Directorate of Technical Development		TBS	Turbo Breech Starter
EE	English Electric		TIRRS	Tornado Infra-red Reconnaissance System
GAF	Government Aircraft Factory		TFU	Telecommunications Flying Unit
GW	Guided Weapon		TSR2	Tactical Strike Reconnaissance 2
IFF	Identification Friend or Foe		UHF	Ultra High Frequency
IRLS	Infra-red Line Scan System		UFO	Unidentified Flying Object
LRCS	Laser Ranging Countermeasures System		VHF	Very High Frequency
LABS	Low Altitude Bombing System		VOR	VHF Omni Directional Aid
LCN	Local Concentration Number		VTOL	Vertical Take-off & Land
MoD(PE)	Ministry of Defence Procurement Executive		WRE	Weapon Research Establishment

Appendix 2 - Canberra Aircraft Leading particulars

Canberra XH568

Type	Canberra B6 Mod
Nose	B2 redesigned forward pressure bulkhead
Fuselage	B6
Tail	B6
Mainplanes	B6
Engines	Avon 109 (ECU 10901)
Starter	Avon 109 TBS 720 Mk3
Undercarriage	Main B6 with Maxarets
	Nose B6
Electrical System	
Generators	Two 9kW Type 519

Canberra WK163

Type	Canberra B6
Nose	B6
Fuselage	B2
Tail	B2
Mainplanes	B6
Engines	Avon 109 (ECU 10901)
Starter	Avon 109 TBS 720 Mk 3
Undercarriage	Main B6 with Maxarets
	Nose B6
Electrical System	
Generators	Two 9kW Type 519

During the 1966 PRC for Canberra WK163 the front fuselage section was brought up to B Mk.6 build standard. Cockpit modifications are shown below.

Starter panel
  Modified to cater for triple breech starters.

Take-off panel
  Standard B6 introduced to cater for management of fuel system, generators and battery control.

Electrical control panel
  Split level modification and wiring changes for B6-type fuel system, starting and air-conditioning.

Pilot's console
  Modified to include engine anti-icing as per B6.

Engine instrument panel
  Modified for B6 type fuel management.

Main electrical panel
  Completely revised to cater for Type 519 generator system as per B6.

Appendix 3 - Canberra Aircraft Movements record of Canberra front fuselage sections

Over the years there has been some confusion surrounding the conversion and fitting of RRE Canberra forward fuselage sections. Whilst many of the type had modifications made to them only the four shown below were exchanged with other airframes of the same type.

SERIAL No.6649 - BASIC B Mk.2

8th October 1968:
  Removed from B Mk.2 WK135

6th February 1969:
  Fitted to airframe centre section B Mk.6 WT327

16th August 1972:
  Removed from WT327

  Converted to hybrid B Mk.6 (long-nose) version

20th March 1975:
  Fitted to airframe centre section B Mk.6 WT333

SERIAL No.71105 - BASIC B Mk.2

10th April 1969:
  Removed from B Mk.2 WG788

  Converted to hybrid B Mk.6 (long-nose) version

3rd September 1970:
  Fitted to airframe centre section B Mk.6 XH568

SERIAL No.71399 - BASIC B Mk.6

10th April 1970:
  Removed from B Mk.6 XH568

15th May 1972:
  Fitted to airframe centre section B Mk.6 WK163

SERIAL No.6663 - BASIC B Mk.2

14th April 1972:
  Removed from B Mk.6 WK163

14th September 1972:
  Fitted to airframe centre section B Mk.6 WT327

Appendix 4
Canberra nose conversions

During the Canberras' service life there were a total of forty-four nose conversions using the reinforced monocoque design. Twenty-four were T Mk.17 ECM conversions for the RAF by English Electric Ltd., Preston. For the purpose of this book only the conversions for R&D, service equipment trials and training uses are recorded.

Short-nose monocoque

Fitting of the short monocoque was sub-contracted by TRE-RRE Aircraft Department under their specification to the Boulton Paul out-station at Defford. The RRE's Aircraft Department manufactured the radome section.

Serial	Mark	Manufacturer	Location	End User
VN828	B2	Boulton Paul	Defford	TRE-RRE
WG789	B2	Boulton Paul	Defford	TRE-RRE
WH660	B2	Boulton Paul	Defford	TRE-RRE
WJ646	B2	Boulton Paul	Defford	TRE-RRE

ELINT modification
WJ775	B6	Boulton Paul	Seighford	51 Sqn
WJ786	B6	Boulton Paul	Seighford	51 Sqn
WT301	B6	Boulton Paul	Seighford	51 Sqn
WT305	B6	Boulton Paul	Seighford	51 Sqn & RRE

Radar Trainer modification
WH714	T11	Boulton Paul	Seighford	228 OCU, 85 Sqn
WH724	T11	Boulton Paul	Seighford	228 OCU, 85, 100 Sqns
WH903	T11	Boulton Paul	Seighford	228 OCU, 85 Sqn
WH904	T11	Boulton Paul	Seighford	228 OCU, 85, 7 Sqns
WJ610	T11	Boulton Paul	Seighford	228 OCU, 85 Sqn
WJ975	T11	Boulton Paul	Seighford	228 OCU, 85, 7, 100 Sqns
WK106	T11	Boulton Paul	Seighford	228 OCU, 85, 100 Sqns
XA536	T11	Boulton Paul	Seighford	228 OCU, 85 Sqn, RRE, 100 Sqn

Both VN828 and WJ646 were operated with the B(I) Mk.8 interdictor forward fuselage suitably converted with the short nose monocoque.

Long-nose monocoque

Four Canberra front fuselages were converted to long-nose configuration. The first was a 'one off' job on WH945 carried out by the RRE Aircraft Department in 1957. Three more conversions followed between 1960 and 1975.

Serial	Mark	Manufacturer	Location	End User
WH945	B6	RRE Aircraft Dept.	Defford	RRE, 97 Sqn
WH953	B6	RRE Aircraft Dept.	Pershore	RRE-DRA
WT333	B6	RRE Aircraft Dept.	Pershore	RRE-DRA
XH568	B6	RRE Aircraft Dept.	Pershore	RRE-DRA

Both WH945 and WH953 had the monocoque conversion fitted to their original forward fuselage.

Appendix 5
Radio and electrical requirements Canberra WK163

Below is an example of how much electrical equipment needed to be fitted to the RRE Canberra fleet to fulfil the requirement for project testing. All items were installed during the aircraft's refurbishment period of 2nd July 1971 to 28th January 1972.

All items marked * are already fitted to the aircraft.
Items marked ** were fitted to the aircraft.

**	Decca Mk.19
	with decimal readout, pictorial display
**	Decca Doppler 62M
**	Marconi 60
*	Sub-miniature Radio Compass
*	ILS
*	Cossor 1600
*	SSR 1600
*	Radar Altimeter Mk.7B
**	Radar Altimeter Mk.6A
*	V/UHF PTR 175
**	UHF PTR 170

Summarised Fit

Communications
  PTR 175
  PTR 170
  Marconi 60
Navigation Aids
  Doppler 62M
  ILS
  Sub Miniature ADF
  Low level Radar Altimeter Mk.7B
  High level Radar Altimeter Mk.6A
  Decca Navigator Mk.19
  G4B Compass System
Secondary Radar
  SSR 1600
Instrument Inverters
  No.1   E184   Flight Instruments
  No.2   RC8A   Emergency Standby
Equipment Inverters
  No.3   E208   Navigational Aids
  No.4   E200   Radar Altimeter Mk.6A
  No.5   Leland   Experimental and Nav Aids
           Standby

Radio and radar equipment total: 11
Supporting installations total: 101

Appendix 6
AS Viper test hours Canberra WK163

Ground Runs			**Flight Tests**		
Date	Time		Date	Time	
Serial No.VP1112			**Serial No.VP1112**		
April 1955					
7th	0.50	Initial Run	16th	1.00	First Flight
13th	0.15		18th	0.50	
14th	0.05		20th	1.10	
16th	0.15		21st	1.55	
			26th	0.40	
			28th	0.30	
			29th	1.05	
May 1955					
5th	0.10		3rd	0.45	
7th	0.10		4th	0.05	
10th	0.30		5th	0.50	
Total	**2.15**		9th	0.45	
			11th	0.55	
			Total	**10.30**	
			Viper Removed		
Serial No.VP1113			**Serial No.VP1113**		
May 1955			*May 1955*		
24th	0.20	Initial Run	25th	0.55	First Flight
25th	0.05		27th	1.55	
26th	0.10				
June 1955					
			1st	0.40	
8th	0.20		2nd	1.10	
14th	0.25		3rd	1.15	
Total	**1.20**		8th	0.05	
			9th	0.30	
			10th	0.55	
			13th	1.00	
			14th	1.35	
			Total	**10.00**	
			Viper Removed		
Serial No.VP1112			**Serial No.VP1112**		
After overhaul			After overhaul		
June 1955					
27th	0.15		30th	0.30	Initial Flight
July 1955					
5th	0.10		5th	0.50	
6th	0.05		6th	0.55	
August 1955					
4th	0.20		5th	1.00	
Total	**0.50**		*Total*	**3.15**	
			Viper Removed		

Plate 47 - Dave Piper leads the Meteor pair into display at the start of Coventry's 'Fifties Festival of Flying' in August 2000.

Display Team

postscript

from the

author's

collection

(Above) Plate 48 - A quite unorthodox view of XH568. The aircraft was last flown in 1996, and has become a main source of spares for WK163.

Plate 49 - Last, but by no means least, CDT's full set of beards is on display alongside WK163 whilst at rest at Biggin Hill in June 1999. From left, Phil Shaw, Roger Joy and Stewart Ross.

Appendix 7
Record of flights from ASM Bitteswell
Canberra WK163

Date	Pilot		Details
28 Jan 1955	P Aked	Woodford	Delivery to Bitteswell
16 Apr 1955	P Aked	Bitteswell	Viper first flight
18 Apr 1955	P Aked	Bitteswell	Flight test
20 Apr 1955	J Bartlam	Bitteswell	Flight test
21 Apr 1955	P Aked	Bitteswell	Flight test
22 Apr 1955	P Aked	Bitteswell	Taxy test
26 Apr 1955	J Bartlam	Bitteswell	Flight test
28 Apr 1955	P Aked	Bitteswell	Flight test
29 Apr 1955	J Bartlam	Bitteswell	Flight test
3 May 1955	P Aked	Bitteswell	Flight test
4 May 1955	P Aked	Bitteswell	To Wattisham and return
5 May 1955	J Bartlam	Bitteswell	Flight test
7 May 1955	J Bartlam	Bitteswell	Handling flight
9 May 1955	A Wittridge	Bitteswell	Flight test
11 May 1955	J Bartlam	Bitteswell	Flight test
25 May 1955	A Wittridge	Bitteswell	Flight test
26 May 1955	P Aked	Bitteswell	Handling flight
27 May 1955	A Wittridge	Bitteswell	Flight test
1 Jun 1955	A Wittridge	Bitteswell	Flight test
2 Jun 1955	P Aked	Bitteswell	Flight test
3 Jun 1955	J Bartlam	Bitteswell	Flight test
6 Jun 1955	H Rayner	Bitteswell	Handling flight
8 Jun 1955	H Rayner	Bitteswell	Flight test
9 Jun 1955	H Rayner	Bitteswell	Flight test
10 Jun 1955	H Rayner	Bitteswell	Flight test
13 Jun 1955	H Rayner	Bitteswell	To Radlett and return
14 Jun 1955	J Bartlam	Bitteswell	Flight test
30 Jun 1955	H Rayner	Bitteswell	Flight test
5 Jul 1955	J Bartlam	Bitteswell	Flight test
6 Jul 1955	J Bartlam	Bitteswell	Flight test
5 Aug 1955	J Bartlam	Bitteswell	Flight test
7 Nov 1955	P Aked	Bitteswell	Post mod flight
8 Nov 1955	A Wittridge	Bitteswell	Handling flight
9 Nov 1955	P Aked	Bitteswell	Handling flight
2 Dec 1955	K Cartwright	Bitteswell	Delivery to Luton

Appendix 8
Scorpion rocket motors tested on WK163

Serial No	Fitted	Removed
Single Motor		
100 series		
NScS1-1 103	18 May 56	24 Jun 56
NScS1-1 104	25 Jun 56	25 Jul 56
Double Motor		
200 series		
NScD 1-2 203	26 Jul 56	23 Nov 56
NScD 1-2 204	24 Nov 56	28 Feb 57
Double Motor		
300 series		
NScD 1-2 302	1 Jun 57	22 Aug 57
NScD 1-2 304	23 Aug 57	2 Sep 57
(Height record gained with motor 304)		
NScD 1-2 302 (refitted after overhaul)	3 Sep 57	11 Sep 57
NScD 1-2 304 (refitted after overhaul)	12 Sep 57	28 Oct 57
NScD 1-2 305	29 Oct 57	16 Apr 58
NScD 1-2 306 (not run or flown)	6 May 58	15 May 58
NScD1-2 305 (not run or flown)	10 Mar 59	16 Mar 59

A total of eight different Scorpion units were flown aboard WK163 resulting in 65 hours of flight testing. The single-motor units were overhauled after one hour flight time, with the double-motor units being overhauled after 1 hour 20 mins flight time.

The dates above are for the initial fitting and removal of motors on WK163.

Select Bibliography

Delve, Green, Clemons
English Electric Canberra
ISBN 0904 597733
Midland Counties Publications 1992

Jones, Barry
English Electric Canberra and Martin B-57
ISBN 1861 262558
Crowood Press 1999

Appendix AP4326F (RRE Modifications)
Canberra B Mk.6 Aircraft

Appendix AP4326B (RRE Modifications)
Canberra B Mk.2 Aircraft

RRE Internal Document Dated 2nd December 1966
Mainplanes Conversion Canberra WK163

RRE Internal Document Dated 15th July 1971
PRC/Installations Programme WK163

RAF Form 700 E
Aircraft Servicing Records
ASM, Napier, RAE, RRE, DRA

RAE (B) Technical Publication 1979
Hybrid Canberra Aircraft

DRA Form AS1
Aircraft Installation Instruction Canberra

RAE (B) Appendix AP1018-0415-15
Aircrew Manual
Canberra Trials Aircraft (long-nose variants)

Pilots Notes Canberra B Mk.2, B Mk.6 Aircraft

Flight Reference Cards
Canberra B Mk.6
Standard & Modified Research Aircraft

RAF Form 707A
Maintenance Record Log
Canberra Trials Aircraft

RAF AP4326F Vol.1
Canberra Aircraft

ASM Bitteswell Airfield Log